Offer Them Life

Offer Them Life

A Life-Based Evangelistic Vision

Dan W. Dunn

WIPF & STOCK · Eugene, Oregon

OFFER THEM LIFE
A Life-Based Evangelistic Vision

Wipf & Stock
An Imprint of Wipf and Stock Publishers
199 W. 8th Ave., Suite 3
Eugene, OR 97401
www.wipfandstock.com

ISBN 13: 978-1-62564-010-9
Manufactured in the U.S.A.

All Scripture quotations are from The Holy Bible, English Standard Version® (ESV®), copyright © 2001 by Crossway, a publishing ministry of Good News Publishers. Used by permission. All rights reserved.

This book is dedicated to the glory of God and the furtherance of God's life-giving intentions in the world through Jesus Christ.
It is also dedicated to my wife and best friend Nancy, who both supported and cheered on this work. We mutually dedicate these pages to those persons who will be reached through the evangelistic ministry of Jesus-followers who live out the implications of a life-based evangelistic vision.

CONTENTS

Preface

OFFER THEM LIFE EXPLORES the implications of having a life-based evangelistic vision. It describes my research into the relationship between a strong emphasis on the biblical theme of life and the theory and practice of Christian evangelism in U.S. America.

In chapter 1, I describe the primary premise of the project, which is that the biblical theme of life may be viewed as one of the primary themes of the Bible, and as such provide a helpful foundation for the theory and practice of evangelism in the U.S. American context. In chapter 2, I more fully develop the theological foundation of my argument, focusing especially on the relationship between the biblical theme of life and the kingdom of God.

In chapters 3 and 4, I share insights gained from selected Old Testament and Johannine scholars who highlight the life theme and other related themes. The focus turns in chapters 5 and 6 to the work of six theologians who either focus on the biblical theme of life or demonstrate a life-oriented anthropological perspective in their theological work. I discuss the eight vital themes that emerged from my study.

I then shift in chapter 7 to the field research component of the project, sharing my discoveries concerning how some Christians conceptualize or experience the role (or lack thereof) of life in evangelistic theory and practice. In chapter 8, I assess the field research data in conjunction with the discoveries I made in the theological and biblical studies materials. Based on this assessment, I share important implications for evangelistic theory and practice that arise from a strong emphasis on the biblical theme of life.

1

Premise and Purpose of This Exploration of a Life-Based Evangelistic Vision

Premise

LIFE MAY BE VIEWED as one of the primary themes of the Bible, and as such provides a helpful foundation for the theory and practice of evangelism in the U.S. American context.[1]

Joseph Dongell proposes that full life be viewed as the macro rubric of Scripture. God is fundamentally the living God (as distinct from other descriptions, such as holy, powerful, or loving). God is vitally alive, and in Christ, God wishes to share this vital experience of life with all of God's creation, including human beings.[2] Hans Klein shares a similar perspective. He contends that the biblical material should be ordered and understood in relation to life (Old Testament) and new life (New Testament).[3]

The nature of the life that Christ offers his followers has vital implications for evangelism. What is the good news that Christians share with non-Christians, and what kind of new life do they invite non-Christians to embrace?[4] George Hunter tells of a young man who once admitted that

1. I describe some of the pertinent characteristics of the U.S. American context later in this chapter.

2. Dongell, Joseph. "Biblical Theology as a Whole." Lecture. Asbury Theological Seminary, Wilmore, KY, May 7, 2009.

3. Klein, "Leben–neues Leben," 91–107.

4. *Non-Christian* or *non-believer* will be used throughout this book to refer to those persons who are not actively and intentionally following Christ. Some scholars prefer the term *pre-Christian* because it honors the fact that most people in the West are outside the influence of Christianity and the church (see Hunter, *How to Reach Secular People*,

he believed in Jesus but had never invited him to be the leader of his life. Hunter asked why this was so, and the young man answered that he had learned in his hometown that opening up to Jesus would result in his becoming some kind of fanatic. Hunter replied, "Look, it just isn't so, and somebody back home once sold you a tragic bill of goods. If you could look into the future and see the man that Christ has in mind for you to be ten years from now, you would stand up and cheer and you would deeply want to be that man. The gospel is not bad news; it is good news. The gospel is congruent with our deepest aspirations for ourselves."[5]

I propose that God created the earth, its animal and plant life, and human beings to experience full, vibrant, vital life in relationship with God and one another, and that this experience of life is what God both makes possible and invites us to embrace in following Jesus Christ. This full life that God offers in Christ is the cornerstone of the good news, and offers a valuable foundation for the theory and practice of evangelism.[6]

Two perspectives underlie the current practice of evangelism in the U.S. American context. The first is one's understanding of eternal life. The second is basing evangelism on the concept of kingdom.

First Perspective: Understanding of Eternal Life

An important issue in this discussion is our understanding of eternal life. In common Christian usage, *eternal* refers to chronological time (forever), so that those who believe in Jesus will live with him throughout eternity after physical death. However, the biblical understanding of eternal life is more than chronological eternity; it also includes a fullness and vitality of

---

13–39). However, in this project I envision the "realm" of evangelism to include not only persons who have little or no knowledge of Christianity (or Christians), but also those who do have knowledge of Christianity (or Christians), and have not yet chosen to become Christ-followers. In this context, *non-Christian* includes but is not limited to those persons whom other scholars would designate as pre-Christian. *Non-believers* will also be used on occasion to honor the Johannine emphasis on believing in Jesus so that we may have life.

5. Hunter, *Church for the Unchurched*, 53.

6. I prefer Dongell's use of *full life* to Klein's use of *new life*. Full life includes new life, but I conceive of it as moving beyond the newness of our life in Christ at the beginning of our relationship with him, which includes relationship with God, other persons, and creation (more will be said on the relational nature of full life in Christ throughout this book), so that it includes a growing awareness and embrace of all that God intends for us in him, throughout our lifetime and into chronological eternity.

life here on this earth. Commenting on John's use of the Greek word for life (*zōe*), one author says that "in most cases it states expressly that the follower of Jesus possesses life even in this world."[7] Rudolf Bultmann agrees. Commenting on a Greek verb cognate of life (*zaō*) in relation to its use in John's Gospel, he writes that "he who believes has *already* passed from death to life."[8] C. H. Dodd shares this perspective, claiming that John offered an addition to the usual Jewish eschatological understanding, so that our post-resurrection life begins not after our resurrection, but rather as a result of our believing in Jesus. Commenting on the Lazarus story, he writes that "the 'resurrection' of which Jesus has spoken is something which may take place before bodily death, and has for its result the possession of eternal life here and now."[9] We see, therefore, that the concept of eternal life includes a life-now dimension as well as a life-then dimension.

If life in Christ is understood primarily in terms of where (or if) we will live during chronological eternity, the focus of evangelism leans toward preparation for life after death. One example of this emphasis is found in the ministry of Evangelism Explosion. In the Evangelism Explosion training material, the two diagnostic questions recommended for Christians to use in witnessing focus on whether the non-Christian will go to heaven. The first question is: "Have you come to a place in your spiritual life where you know for certain that if you were to die today you would go to heaven, or is that something you would say you're still working on?"[10] The second question asks: "Suppose you were to die today and stand before God and He were to say to you, 'Why should I let you into My heaven?' What would you say?"[11] This focus continues in the section describing the essential gospel to be shared, which is summarized as follows: Heaven is a free gift; it is not earned or deserved; people are sinners and cannot save themselves; God is both merciful and just, so God came down into human flesh, died on the cross and rose from the dead to pay the penalty for our sins and to purchase a place in heaven for us.[12] Of particular note is the statement that

---

7. Danker, *Greek-English Lexicon*, 430.

8. Bultmann, "ζαω," 870.

9. Dodd, *Interpretation of the Fourth Gospel*, 148.

10. Kennedy, *Evangelism Explosion*, 32.

11. Ibid., 33.

12. Ibid., 33–36.

"the whole Bible is about one great transaction . . . By His grace He freely offers to give to us this gift of heaven."[13]

This strong emphasis on the everlasting nature of the life that Christ makes possible for us in heaven is an appropriate focus for the theory and practice of evangelism. Christians should be motivated by a strong interest in helping persons live forever with Christ, and ministries that are effective in sharing this dimension of the gospel are to be encouraged. This is especially true of ministries that have a strong follow-up process to help new believers move from the getting-to-heaven focus toward a focus on a thriving life of discipleship. In this regard, one may agree with George Sweazey, who notes that as long as a congregation is effective in helping Christians grow in their experience of the many dimensions of life in God's grace, they "can safely make their first appeal through just one aspect of the gospel."[14] Some congregations, however, may find it difficult to make their discipleship and follow-up ministries broader than their evangelism ministries. The dimension(s) of the gospel on which they focus in their evangelism may tend(s) to be the dimension(s) that take(s) precedence in the rest of their ministries.[15]

Evangelism in the U.S. American context, therefore, should not limit itself to the heavenly dimension of the good news of Jesus Christ. This is especially true when one considers that Christian evangelizing must attend to questions and issues that people are actually addressing, rather than those that Christians think they are (or should be) addressing.[16] It is here that

13. Kennedy, *Evangelism Explosion*, 34–35.

14. Sweazey, *Effective Evangelism*, 60.

15. As one example, Evangelism Explosion engages in a follow-up process in which a life of discipleship is encouraged, but this new life of discipleship is predicated on the evangelistic emphasis on heaven. Thus, discipleship is fueled by our gratitude for the gift of heaven ("The reason for living a godly life is gratitude . . . I'm saying 'thank you' for the gift of eternal life Christ has given me." Kennedy, *Evangelism Explosion*, 49). This is an appropriate focus, but it is also a limiting focus that makes it difficult for persons to capture and experience the full-life dimensions of Christian living.

16. Leslie Newbigin argues against this perspective in *The Gospel in a Pluralistic Society*. He suggests that to address ourselves to questions the world is asking does not serve well because "the world's questions are not the questions which lead to life" (119). I agree with Newbigin's sentiment here. However, I also concur with other writers who claim that some of the best starting points for relationships with non-Christians are related to questions that those non-Christians are asking. I do not suggest that we should be bound by their questions, but that we should at least be aware of them and know that they can sometimes provide points of identification and entry into conversation and/or relationship. Given the strong individualistic focus in U.S. American culture, it is likely that most non-believers will first be motivated to consider the Christ-following journey based on

a stronger emphasis on the biblical theme of life can inform evangelistic efforts, for people today have far more interest in whether they can experience life now than in whether (or where) they will live for chronological eternity.[17]

Some of the questions we should attend to in evangelistic theory and practice are:

- In what ways are people seeking life today?

- How much does their battle against death take away from their experience of full life?

- If we assume that they are seeking life, do we make a corollary assumption that their daily experience is more akin to death?

- If so, who or what are the "thieves" that are trying to steal and kill and destroy their lives (based on the language of John 10:10)?

Christians, therefore, must continually discern ways of thinking about and practicing evangelism that honor the strong biblical theme that God wants God's created humanity to experience life fully (abundantly, according to John 10:10), on this earth, prior to physical death.

When evangelism deals with sin, for example, mutual emphasis could be given to the life-forever benefits of being forgiven through Christ (e.g., access to heaven) and to the life-now benefits of Christ's forgiveness (e.g., freedom from bondage).[18] Likewise, evangelism could endeavor to discover

---

appeal to their own self-interest. As Steward and Bennett contend in *American Cultural Patterns*, one result of the U.S. American focus on individualism is "an intense self-centeredness" (63). In this context, to expect non-Christians to be initially motivated by questions that they do not see as being relevant to them in some way is simply unrealistic.

17. Donald Soper has observed in *Advocacy of the Gospel* that as a result of the process of secularity, five shifts took place in the Western world. One of these shifts was from a death orientation to a life orientation. People no longer think about death on such a large scale as they once did. There is a far greater emphasis on life. Soper maintains that we must bear this in mind as we advocate the good news of Jesus Christ. "If we talk about eternal life, as under God we are compelled to do when we preach, we must talk about the present possibility which our blessed Lord advocated and himself spoke of" (17–18). Soper's insights are almost fifty years old, but they remain true even today, as confirmed in Charles Taylor's much more recent work. In *A Secular Age*, Taylor notes that "modern humanism tends to develop a notion of human flourishing which has no place for death" and that death "must be combated, and held off till the very last moment" (320).

18. John Wesley addresses this in an indirect way with the distinction he makes between justification and the new birth. He writes that "God in justifying us does something *for* us; in begetting us again, he does the work *in* us. The former changes our outward relation to God, so that of enemies we become children; by the latter our inmost souls are

appropriate means for expressing how deeply God is for humanity while at the same time honoring that God is against sin. Similarly, repentance could be accentuated as an important dimension of "getting right with God" in order to prepare oneself for life in the hereafter, but it could also be stressed as a contributing factor to reconciliation and full enjoyment of relationships with people here on earth. The same point could be illustrated in relation to other theological concepts, such as atonement, redemption, salvation, and justification. In evangelism, each of these concepts could be expressed in ways that would honor both the life-after-death and the life-before-death benefits of following Christ.

Current evangelism in the United States does not completely ignore the impact of Christ-following during this lifetime. However, some of the common ways that evangelism portrays the benefits of Christ-following during this lifetime fall short of the fully orbed life God intends God's followers to experience. Two U.S. American portraits of Christian living in particular come to mind: the prosperity gospel and the "you'll never have another problem" gospel.[19]

The prosperity gospel speaks to abundant living on this side of death; however, some of its proponents do so in biblically and theologically inappropriate ways. There is too much emphasis on financial well-being and too little emphasis on other dimensions of God-intended human fullness, such as servanthood, mutuality in helping other people thrive, and relational community. I will deal more fully with the prosperity gospel in a subsequent chapter.

The "you'll never have another problem" gospel obviously communicates that following Christ brings blessings in this life, but it just as obviously promises something that cannot be delivered, something God neither promises nor intends.[20] You need only consider the "hall of faith"

changed, so that of sinners we become saints. The one restores us to the favour, the other to the image, of God. The one is the taking away the guilt, the other the taking away the power, of sin . . . " Wesley, *The Works of John Wesley*, 224.

19. In discussing the prosperity gospel, I prefer Gordon Fee's description in *The Disease of the Health & Wealth Gospels* (2–3) that the primary affirmation of the prosperity gospel is that "God wills the (financial) prosperity of every one of his children, and therefore for a Christian to be in poverty is to be outside God's intended will." A related secondary affirmation that is often implied or stated outright is that "the King's kids . . . should always go first-class."

20. It is difficult to locate examples in print for citation purposes of no-more-problems evangelism. George Hunter observes that this kind of message usually gets communicated when preachers get carried away in their evangelistic communication, but

in Hebrews 11 to discern that faithfulness in following God's way does not guarantee problem-free living. An important issue that is addressed in this book, therefore, is that some evangelistic theory and practice do not sufficiently appreciate and incorporate the biblical theme of full life in Christ, particularly in relation to God's intention for us to experience fullness of life here on earth, prior to physical death.

Second Perspective: Basing Evangelism on "Kingdom"

The foundational premise of this project is that evangelistic theory and practice should be grounded in the biblical theme of life. How, therefore, does the strong synoptic emphasis on the kingdom of God fit into this picture? One may consider, for example, the proposal from William Abraham that evangelism is best understood as "that set of intentional activities governed by the goal of initiating persons into the kingdom of God for the first time."[21] With his emphasis on initiation into the kingdom of God, Abraham seeks to honor the strong prevalence of kingdom language in the Bible, particularly in regard to the teachings of Jesus. Furthermore, he wants to distinguish between initiating persons into the kingdom and initiating them into the church. This helps us move from an anthropocentric focus on "what we do" or on "what is done to us" in the church's initiation process to a theocentric focus "on the majestic and awesome activity of a Trinitarian God whose actions on our behalf stagger our imagination and dissolve into impenetrable mystery."[22]

Grounded in this comprehensive kingdom-based understanding, Abraham extracts three principles that are vital for the ministry of evangelism. First, evangelism is inextricably linked with worship in the Christian community. Second, the good news of the kingdom must be proclaimed. Third, some form of the catechumenate should be reinstated in order to help kingdom initiates understand and embrace all the dimensions of kingdom initiation.[23]

Scott Jones offers a different portrayal of evangelism. He insists that evangelism should be theologically grounded in what has become known

---

they seldom include it in written works (email message to author, February 19, 2010).

21. Abraham, *Logic of Evangelism*, 95.

22. Ibid., 98.

23. Ibid., 167–80.

as Jesus's Great Commandment, to love God and neighbor.[24] Jones suggests that loving God and neighbor is central to God's intentions for us and as such must be given the highest priority in evangelism. It is out of love for us and all of God's creation that God came to earth as Jesus and announced the reign of God. Furthermore, the appropriate way to respond to God's reign is to be a practicing disciple. Thus, it is through discipleship that we best learn and practice the love of God, neighbor, and self.[25] Evangelism, therefore, "is that set of loving, intentional activities governed by the goal of initiating persons into Christian discipleship in response to the reign of God."[26]

Jones refers to the initiation of persons into Christian discipleship in response to the reign of God, whereas Abraham refers to initiating them into the reign (kingdom) of God itself. They both include the kingdom theme in their theological vision for evangelism. Given the strong presence of the kingdom theme in the Synoptic Gospels, this is not surprising in the least, and to a certain extent this is helpful. Inclusion of the kingdom theme in evangelistic thought reminds us that the primary role of evangelism is to partner with the Holy Spirit in guiding, leading, and inviting people toward God's intentions for them. For Abraham, God's intentions for us revolve around God's kingdom, whereas for Jones those intentions revolve around the love of God, self, and others that becomes possible through Christian discipleship.

It is not my purpose to engage in a point-by-point debate with Jones and Abraham concerning their evangelistic visions. Furthermore, there is much to value in each of their visions. There is no question that Jones is correct in insisting that evangelism must move persons toward discipleship, and that this discipleship must be grounded in the love of God, which is a foundational characteristic of God. Likewise, Abraham's desire to honor the kingdom theme in the Bible and to avoid undue focus on introducing persons to the institutional church is an appropriate emphasis. There is, however, another theme that is prior to their themes of choice: life. God's reign as both embodied and proclaimed by Jesus is vitally important to the biblical portrayal, and so too is a life of discipleship grounded in love; but each of these may be appropriately viewed in relation to the foundational

24. Varying versions of the Great Commandment are found in Matt 22:37–39, Mark 12:28–34, and Luke 10:27–28.

25. Jones, *Evangelistic Love of God and Neighbor*, 13–18, 50–65, 99.

26. Ibid., 18.

theme of life. I do not suggest that the evangelistic visions of Jones and Abraham are incorrect or less valuable than a life-based one. A life-based evangelistic vision, however, is equally as valuable as theirs. Furthermore, a life-based evangelistic vision is biblically and theologically prior to those based in God's reign or kingdom, for creation of life takes place in the biblical narrative far sooner than any mention of God's kingdom or reign.[27]

Purpose

The purpose of this project is to discern the evangelistic implications that arise from a strong focus on the biblical theme of life in its God-intended fullness.

Four clusters of questions are of particular interest regarding the implications of a life-based evangelistic vision. The first cluster pertains to the gospel. What is the good news? What is good about the good news? In inviting others to Christ, what is it that we are inviting non-Christians toward? What are we asking them to embrace? To what extent does our full-life understanding influence our communication of the good news?[28] If it is included in our gospel communication, is it also included in the invitation that is extended to non-Christians?

A second cluster of questions relates to the essential meaning of the biblical theme of life. What does life mean? What kind of life does God intend for men and women? What does God do to offer us full life? What do human beings need to do to appropriate or access full life? How might we lose this life? What perspectives do we gain from Old Testament scholars

27. As a person steeped in the Wesleyan tradition, I find it encouraging that Steve Harper links much of Wesleyan theology with a focus on life. When presenting foundational Wesleyan concepts in seminars or workshops, he divides them into three main categories: (a) the message of life (grace); (b) the means to life (the means of grace); and (c) the mission for life. A further delineation is made within each of these three categories. The *message of life* involves (a) prevenient grace (the invitation to life); (b) converting grace, (the entrance into life); (c) sanctifying grace (the consecration of life); and (d) glorifying grace (the transition to everlasting life). The *means of life* include (a) instituted means and (b) prudential means. The *mission for life* comprises (a) redeem the lost, (b) renew the church, and (c) reform the nation (Steve Harper, personal conversation, April 27, 2011).

28. For example, a person may claim to believe in full life in Christ. Their use of the "Bridge Method" in their gospel presentations, a method that focuses on the chasm between unredeemed humanity and God, may, however, represent a lack of connection between theological belief and gospel presentation.

who value the life theme? What does the prevalence of the life theme in John's Gospel mean?[29]

A third cluster of questions has to do with the relationship between the biblical themes of life, the kingdom of God (especially in the Synoptic Gospels), and eternal life (especially in John). Given the strong emphasis of Jesus on the kingdom of God in the Synoptic Gospels, would one say that the biblical theme of life is somehow subservient to the kingdom theme, vice versa, or is there another way to conceptualize that relationship? Since John's Gospel virtually ignores kingdom language and strongly emphasizes the language of life, especially eternal life, might we conceive of the kingdom and eternal life as two ways to express the same truth(s), or are they separate yet related dimensions of the gospel; or something else?

A fourth cluster of questions deals with the relational dimensions of full life in Christ. What is the relationship between my experience of full life in Christ and your experience of it? Can a person experience this life outside of relationship? How predominantly does full life in Jesus flow along relational lines to reach those who do not yet follow him? How privatized can evangelism be? How communal should it be?

Philip Potter believes that the experience of full life cannot be privatized, but must include participation in extending that full life to others. According to his biographer, Potter believes that "the way of Christ (an open door) is always to welcome and enable others to share in a full life."[30] Rodney Stark underscores this issue as well, claiming that "the basis for successful conversionist movements is growth through social networks, through a *structure of direct and intimate interpersonal attachments*."[31] An important claim in this book, therefore, is that full life in Christ cannot be experienced, expressed, or shared outside the scope of relationships, nor at the expense of other persons.

The U.S. American Context of the Study

The scope of this project is limited to the U.S. American context. Given the complexity of U.S. American demographics and the presence of multiple ways of seeing the world, it is difficult (if not impossible) to describe the

---

29. I focus on John's Gospel in this book because of his pervasive and consistent references to life.

30. Jagessar, *Full Life for All*, 123.

31. Stark, *The Rise of Christianity*, 20.

U.S. American context. There are a great many ethnic and linguistic expressions represented in the United States. Additionally, there are varying worldviews that shape how persons see and respond to the world. There is a vast array of literature, for example, concerning modern, postmodern, and post-postmodern worldview dynamics.[32] Moreover, some scholars believe that generational differences can enlighten us concerning cultural and/or worldview variations, so that in recent years words such as *Boomers, Millennials,* and *Xers* have crept into our vocabulary.[33] Additionally, we could point to the divergent political views that are represented in the United States, as well as the broad array of religious (or irreligious) perspectives. Any perceptive observer of the U.S. American context will understand that it includes a diverse representation of many viewpoints.

In spite of this divergent scene, however, there is a consistent coherence among certain key elements of how Americans in general think and act in their daily lives. Robert Bellah, for example, suggests that through the "institutions" of the state and the free enterprise market, by way of their "agencies" of television and education, "there is an enormously powerful common culture in America."[34] Gary Althen and Janet Bennett note that even though there is wide-ranging diversity in the U.S. American context, when one compares U.S. Americans with people from other nations (such as the Japanese, for example), "it becomes clear that certain attitudes and behaviors are much more characteristic of the Americans and others are far more typical of the Japanese."[35] Claude Fischer writes that in spite of the "changes, spikes, sideways moves, and reversals" that may be discerned in U.S. history, "continuity is a striking feature of American culture," so that "what seemed socially distinctive about America in the eighteenth century still seems distinctive in the twenty-first."[36]

32. Paul Hiebert, for example, in *Transforming Worldviews* (105–264) writes about the different dynamics involved in the worldview of small-scale oral societies, the peasant worldview, the modern worldview, the postmodern worldview, and the post-postmodern worldview.

33. A few examples of literature relating to different generations in America include the following: Howe and Strauss, *Millennials Rising*; Smith and Clurman, *Generation Ageless*; Hanson, *Baby Boomers and Beyond*; Erickson, *What's Next, Gen X?*; and Dyck, *Generation Ex-Christian*. This is obviously not an exhaustive list, but is sufficient to confirm that generational differences are an important dynamic in the U.S. American context.

34. Bellah, "Is There a Common American Culture?" 614–6.

35. Althen and Bennett, *American Ways*, xxii.

36. Fischer, *Made in America*, 241.

This does not mean that all Americans think and act precisely the same. There is variation, uniqueness, and divergence. And yet there are also some deep-seated convictions and behavioral tendencies that permeate much of the U.S. American context.[37] The available literature about U.S. American cultural tendencies illustrates a large number of things that one might say are important for understanding the U.S. American context.[38] To be as concise as possible, however, I will limit my comments to the two cultural dimensions that are most pertinent to this project. At later points in the book, I will introduce additional U.S. American tendencies that are germane to specific topics being discussed at those times.

By far, the most pervasive and impactful dimension of the U.S. American context is the passionate stress on individualism. Robert Bellah talks about the strong emphasis in the United States on the "sacredness of the individual conscience, the individual person." He traces this emphasis back to the sectarian religious groups that landed on American shores in the seventeenth century. They brought an intense commitment to "the absolute centrality of religious freedom, of the sacredness of individual conscience in matters of religious belief."[39] Since that time, the emphasis on individualism has expanded to include not only a focus on individual conscience, but also on an understanding of the individual self as distinct and unique. In this regard, Steward and Bennett write, "Americans naturally assume that each person is not only a separate biological entity, but also a unique psychological being and a singular member of the social order," so that "me and my" is "one of the sharpest dichotomies of American culture."[40] Asitimbay asserts

37. Though I have been exposed to a great deal of anthropological and sociological research, these are not my fields of expertise. I will not, therefore, attempt any strict definitions of culture, worldview, and the like. For the purpose of this book, I am focusing primarily on the simple yet important dimensions of how U.S. Americans think and act.

38. Following are a few examples of themes that are highlighted in the literature. Althen and Bennett (*American Ways*, 4) highlight eight primary categories: (1) individualism, freedom, competitiveness, and privacy; (2) equality; (3) informality; (4) the future, change, and progress; (5) goodness of humanity; (6) time (lineal); (7) achievement, action, work, and materialism; and (8) directness and assertiveness. Claude Fischer (*Made in America*, ix, 8–9) lifts up voluntarism (a combination of individualism and commitment to voluntary groups [more on this later]) as the most distinctive element of U.S. American culture, but also stresses the role of security, material goods, and self-perfecting. Steward and Bennett (*American Cultural Patterns*, 33–74) mention several of the themes that are highlighted by Althen and Bennett, plus they refer to pragmatism, null logic, causation, achievement, and time thrift.

39. Bellah, "Is There a Common American Culture?" 617.

40. Steward and Bennett, *American Cultural Patterns*, 129.

that one of the reasons this individual stress is so robust in the United States is that Americans are immersed in this reality from a very early age. She notes that "the notion of individual needs coming before the needs of others is taught before you can even talk." Moreover, children are taught that they have freedom to make choices. "You choose. This is what you hear, like an echo, from every corner of the United States."[41] Individualism is a driving force (most likely *the* driving force) of U.S. American culture. You will encounter multiple references to the impact of individualism in this book.[42]

The second dimension of the U.S. American context that is germane to this project is privacy, and it grows out of the emphasis on individualism. Because we conceive of the individual self as a distinct and unique entity, we also therefore view ourselves as separate from all others, and hence we attach a strong value to privacy. Since we are different from everyone else and have our own unique identity, we "tend to assume that most people 'need some time to themselves' . . . to think about things or recover their spent psychological energy."[43] We have already noted that individualism makes it difficult for people to respond fully to God's intentions for them to live as relational beings. In a similar fashion, privacy makes it challenging for people to embrace God's intentions for their Christ-following journey to impact the exterior, public spaces of their lives. The public impact of the full life that God intends for us in Jesus will be addressed more fully later in this book.

41. Asitimbay, *What's Up America?* 9.

42. To cite just one example, individualism influences how willing (or able) U.S. Americans are to respond to the idea that God created us to be relational and social beings, and this impacts our understanding of the vital role of participation in communities of faith as integral to our Christ-following journey.

43. Althen and Bennett, *American Ways*, 11.

2

Theological Foundation More Fully Developed

Tension between the "Already" and the "Not Yet" of the Kingdom

THE SYNOPTIC GOSPELS PRESENT the kingdom as a primary focus of Jesus's ministry. Mark shows Jesus's public ministry commencing with the announcement that "the time is fulfilled, and the kingdom of God is at hand; repent and believe in the gospel."[1] Matthew portrays a similar beginning after Jesus's wilderness experience, noting that "from that time Jesus began to preach, saying, 'Repent, for the kingdom of heaven is at hand.'"[2] Luke introduces Jesus's connection with kingdom thinking even before Jesus's birth, as the angel Gabriel tells Mary that the child to whom she will give birth "will reign over the house of Jacob forever, and of his kingdom there will be no end."[3]

The importance of kingdom to Jesus's ministry and teaching is seldom in dispute. However, Jesus's kingdom imagery has been interpreted in a wide variety of ways through the years. One of the most important is whether and/or when the kingdom of God will be (or has been) fulfilled.

---

1. Mark 1:15.

2. Matt 4:17. Although some scholars believe that Matthew's designation of the kingdom of *heaven* should be interpreted differently than the designation of the kingdom of *God* in Mark and Luke, most scholars believe these designations refer to the same symbolic concept. In "Kingdom of God/Kingdom of Heaven," Caragounis, for example, says that the "equivalence" of these two designations "is indicated by their content, context and interchangeability in the Gospels" (417).

3. Luke 1:33.

Albert Schweitzer, for example, believed that Jesus was originally awaiting a kingdom consummation in some sort of *parousia*. When that failed to materialize, Jesus and his followers began to reformulate their views about the kingdom's nearness, pushing the coming of the kingdom out to the future. Schweitzer follows the lead of the "thoroughgoing eschatological school," noting that "the whole history of 'Christianity' down to the present day, that is to say, the real inner history of it, is based on the 'delay of the parousia.'"[4]

C. H. Dodd, on the other hand, believed that the predominant lens through which we should view Jesus's kingdom language is that of "realized eschatology," by which he meant that "it is not that the Kingdom of God will shortly come, but that it is a present fact."[5] This perspective led Dodd to interpret most of Jesus's kingdom-related parables as focusing on present impact rather than referring to future events. Thus, in commenting on the four "parables of crisis"[6] ("therefore keep watch"), Dodd observes that "it seems possible, therefore, to give to all these 'eschatological' parables an application within the context of the ministry of Jesus. They were intended to enforce His appeal to men [*sic*] to recognize that the Kingdom of God was present in all its momentous consequences, and that by their conduct in the presence of this tremendous crisis they would judge themselves as faithful or unfaithful, wise or foolish."[7]

For Dodd, therefore, the kingdom had already arrived in the person and ministry of Jesus. For Schweitzer the kingdom had not yet made its appearance or reached its fulfillment.

A large number of scholars today prefer to include both of these dimensions in their thinking about the kingdom, so that they reach what Caragounis calls "mediating positions according to which the kingdom of God is conceived as both present and future."[8] The basic concept is that in Jesus the kingdom has already come, as validated by his miracles (especially his power over Satan), confirmed through his sacrificial death (a coronation of sorts), and vindicated through his resurrection; and yet the

---

4. Schweitzer, *Quest of the Historical Jesus*, 328.

5. Dodd, *Parables of the Kingdom*, 143.

6. The Faithful and Unfaithful Servants (Matt 24:45–51 and Luke 12:42–46); The Waiting Servants (Mark 13:33–37 and Luke 12:35–38); The Thief at Night (Matt 24:43–44 and Luke 12:39–40); and The Ten Virgins (Matt 25:1–13).

7. Dodd, *Parables of the Kingdom*, 138–9.

8. Caragounis, "Kingdom of God/Kingdom of Heaven," 421.

final fulfillment of the kingdom is still to come in the end times with the parousia and the great wedding banquet of the Lamb.

There is a wide variety of perspectives on how one might conceive of the balance or tension between the already and the not-yet of kingdom fulfillment. Beasley-Murray writes that "the believer's experience of grace is set between an accomplished redemption and an awaited consummation."[9] Kummel prefers to think of the kingdom as being expected in the near future (and therefore not yet here), so that Jesus's miracles served as "premonitory signs in the present." Yet he notes that there is also a sense in which the kingdom is already present in Jesus, the Strong Man. The tension, therefore, lies between the promise of a future consummation of history and the fulfillment of that history in Jesus.[10]

Cullman grounds his views in the understanding of time among early Christians, who thought not in terms of "the spatial contrast between the Here and the Beyond, but from the time distinction between Formerly and Now and Then."[11] This means that the Judaic view of two ages (this age and the age to come) has been altered in Christianity, for Jesus has divided time in a fresh way, having become the center of the age to come. Believers, therefore, know that although the war is still being fought, the decisive battle has already been won.[12]

These examples serve to illustrate that a great deal of material has been written on the theme of the already and not-yet character of the kingdom's fulfillment.[13] For my purposes, the most important factor to note is how

9. Beasley-Murray, *Jesus and the Kingdom of God*, 338.

10. Kummel, *Promise and Fulfillment*, 21, 109, 155.

11. Cullman, *Christ and Time*, 37.

12. Ibid., 81–87.

13. As one might imagine, much has been written concerning other dimensions of the kingdom too, with a broad variance of perspectives. Perrin, for example, building on his own work in biblical studies plus the work of Philip Wheelwright in *Metaphor and Reality*, contends that the kingship-of-God myth in ancient Israel led to the emergence of the symbol of the kingdom of God, and that Jesus's use of this symbol is *tensive* (carries a wide range of meanings) rather than *steno* (a more fixed meaning). To interpret the kingdom symbol in the New Testament, therefore, one must consider whether the kingship-of-God myth has meaning to those who hear Jesus's use of the kingdom of God symbol, and what that symbol might evoke in the hearers in relation to that myth (Perrin, *Jesus and the Language of the Kingdom*, especially 1–45; 202). Bock, however, is uncomfortable with Perrin's insistence that all of Jesus's kingdom language is tensive, so he argues in "The Kingdom of God in New Testament Theology" that Jesus's kingdom language was tensive but built on a stable (steno) base (36). From a completely different perspective, Houtepen in "Apocalyptics and the Kingdom of God" refers to the kingdom

the tension between the already and not-yet dimensions of kingdom fulfill-ment relates to the biblical theme of life, and then consequently how this relates to the theory and practice of evangelism. *Tension* is the critical word here, for it helps us understand that the dynamic more appropriately has to do with the tension between the both–and of the already and not-yet dimensions of the kingdom than with any attempt to choose between these two dimensions in an either–or way.[14] James Dunn suggests that Paul sees an eschatological gap opening up with Jesus, so that the starting point of the future age has been "pulled back into the present age, to begin with Christ's resurrection" and the "distinctive feature of Paul's theology is *not* the eschatology, but the *tension* which his revised eschatology sets up."[15] Peter Davids also characterizes the already and not-yet dynamic as a ten-sion, observing that "the king may have come, but he is still coming. The kingdom is already here in the presence of the king, but the kingdom has not yet arrived."[16] Bosch shares these sentiments, and he helpfully notes that not only is this tension unresolved in Jesus's usage (he prefers the des-ignation of reign of God), but should remain that way, for "it is precisely *in* this creative tension that the reality of God's reign has significance for our contemporary mission."[17]

In keeping with the spirit of Bosch, I suggest that the tension between the already and not-yet dimensions of kingdom fulfillment bears a strong relationship to the biblical theme of life. Recognizing this tension prompts

more as a prophetic reality than an apocalyptic one, and speaks of "eschatological on-tology" in terms of God as "creative advance" (291–311). Waltke in "'The Kingdom of God in Biblical Theology" speaks of the kingdom in terms of God's establishment of his *moral* rule, and then discusses the four related primary Old Testament themes (common people, land, law, ruler), and how those themes were reinterpreted in the New Testa-ment (15–27). I could give a myriad of other illustrations, but these suffice to portray the broad diversity of views related to the kingdom of God. My project is not finally about the kingdom of God but about the evangelistic implications of a strong emphasis on the biblical theme of life. Thus I want to limit my focus in the theological foundation to the relationship between the already and not-yet dimensions of kingdom fulfillment, the biblical theme of life, and evangelism.

14. O. V. Jathanna in "Jesus Christ—The Life of the World" addresses the tension by suggesting that "life" is an "intensive metaphor," which means that its meaning goes beyond both the literal and metaphorical associations of the term. "It refers to what is transcendentally and eschatologically real—i.e., in view of reality-as-it-should-be and reality-as-it-will-be, and in the proleptic event of Christ reality-as-it-already-is" (78).

15. Dunn, *Theology of Paul the Apostle*, 464–5.

16. Davids, "The Kingdom of God Come with Power," 19.

17. Bosch, *Transforming Mission*, 32.

us to ask: Has the kingdom come fully enough in Jesus that we can experience the life that God intends for us when we submit to Jesus's reign and rule, or, is it only possible to experience partial life in Christ because the kingdom's fullness remains to be seen at some future time?

The tension between the already and not-yet dimensions of kingdom fulfillment helps us understand that while there is a certain measure of life that we will only be able to experience in the future, there is also a vibrant fullness of life that can be experienced now. It's not that we receive a little bit of life now and then at a later point we will receive eternal life; we receive eternal life now. We receive the very Spirit of God. We are renewed in Christ and the Spirit. We are transformed. We are made alive in a way we neither experienced nor understood before.

Is this transformation made instantaneously complete? Not at all. What has begun is a process of transformation that will endure a lifetime and beyond, into chronological eternity. However, our incomplete transformation is not because we receive an incomplete (or insufficient) life, but because the two ages (the old age and the age to come) overlap. It is not that we have been given only partial life in Christ, but rather that the full life in Christ that is ours is "crowded out" and "cluttered" by the old age.

Please note: I am not proposing a reformulation of the no-more-problems version of the gospel. I affirm the truth that we will not experience the complete and final fullness of God-intended life prior to our own death. We will continue to struggle with sin, illness, sickness, and death. This is due to the fact that we are living between the times. We are living in the overlap of the old age and the age to come.[18] We cannot (nor should not) do away with the tension between these two ages. However, too many Christians erroneously assume that the tension is between a fully powerful-and-present old age and a partially powerful-and-present age to come. Thus, the biblical and theological concern here is that we not undermine or minimize the fullness of what God has done in Christ. The new age (the age to come) has come in its fullness. We have already received the possibility of new life in Christ in full measure. The reason we sometimes do not yet experience the full measure of this new life is that we live in the overlap between the old age and the age to come, and thus, the complete destruction of the old age has not yet taken place.[19]

18. For an excellent treatment of the tension created by this overlap, see Dunn, *Theology of Paul the Apostle*, 461–98.

19. Another factor involved in our less-than-full experience of life on earth is that we

It is also not that we live in some third age in which the fullness of life is weaker than it will be in the age to come. Rather, it is that the old age continues to exert its influence and power, or as Dallas Willard phrases it, "*other* 'kingdoms' are still present on earth along with the kingdom of the heavens."[20] These other kingdoms play a role in the extent to which we experience the full measure of life that God's kingdom brings, but their presence does not mean that God's kingdom has only come in partial measure.[21]

Thus, instead of focusing on the impossibility of experiencing full life in Christ due to the presence and power of the old age, Christians, in both discipleship and evangelism, should focus on the possibility of experiencing full life in Jesus due to the presence and power of the age to come.

In this recommendation I do not assume that the ministry of evangelism will deliver full God-intended life-in-Jesus, for that is more appropriately the role of the ministry of discipleship. I do, however, suggest that the ministry of evangelism should cast the vision of the full God-intended life-in-Jesus. This is more faithful to the core message of the good news of the gospel, it helps non-Christians more fully understand what they are being invited to embrace (on the front end of their journey), and it more appropriately "sets up" the ministry of discipleship by providing a more complete biblical frame of reference for the full life that discipleship is to help us grow into.

Life Is Central: It Is God's Prior Intent

You might surmise from this discussion that the kingdom provides the foundation for an understanding of life. To a certain extent this is true. The prevalence of kingdom language in the Synoptic Gospels prompts us to

---

are created as finite beings. I will deal with this topic in chapter 5, using insights from David Kelsey (who speaks of living on "borrowed breath") and Karl Barth (who talks about the provisional nature of our life in Christ).

20. Willard, *Divine Conspiracy*, 29.

21. Perhaps a similar belief in the fullness of God's kingdom that was present in Jesus's life, ministry, death, and resurrection is what led John Wesley to believe in Christian perfection to the extent that he did. He acknowledged that Christians are not exempt "either from ignorance, or mistake, or infirmities, or temptations," due to their continued presence in the old age; and yet because they also experience the full power of the age to come, "Christians are saved in this world from all sin, from all unrighteousness; that they are now in such a sense perfect, as not to commit sin, and to be freed from evil thoughts and evil tempers" (Wesley, "Christian Perfection," 1–19).

consider the kingdom to be a central (for some people, *the* central) theme for biblical and theological work. However, a strong case can be made from a different perspective: the biblical theme of life could also quite legitimately serve as the central organizing principle of the Bible.

Several Old Testament scholars highlight the importance of life in the Bible. As mentioned in chapter 1, Hans Klein postulates that the Old Testament focuses on life and the New Testament on new life. Edmond Jacob notes that "the idea of eternity is secondary to that of life. God is not living because he is eternal, but he is eternal because he is living."[22] Otto Baab observes that the designation of God as living (or alive) is attached more than sixty times to formulaic oaths that include God's name.[23] Eichrodt refers to two leading motifs regarding the Jewish attitude to the defeat of death. One relates to "the conquest of death as an eschatological event."[24] The second refers to the belief that prior to history's end there is a sense in which, through our relationship (encounter) with God, life "acquires an indestructible content."[25] Eichrodt notes that we are speaking not so much of resurrection as we are of the realization that included in our life with God is an understanding that God provides a life-filled yes to God's worshippers. This yes provides the God-follower with a vision and experience of life that supersedes whatever may happen in physical death.

John's Gospel offers insightful perspectives on the life theme too. Raymond E. Brown suggests that "the Fourth Gospel may be called the Gospel of life,"[26] and Rudolf Schnackenburg remarks that "everything the Johannine Jesus says and does, all that he reveals and all that he accomplishes as 'signs', takes place in view of man's [*sic*] attaining salvation, in view of his gaining divine life."[27] D. Moody Smith concurs, writing that "the eschatological goal, the essence of salvation, according to the Fourth Gospel is life."[28] Finally, Leon Morris writes that John's purpose is to convince his readers that Jesus is the Christ, "in order that he may bring them to a place of faith and accordingly to new life in Christ's name."[29]

22. Jacob, *Theology of the Old Testament*, 38.

23. Baab, *Theology of the Old Testament*, 26.

24. Eichrodt, *Theology of the Old Testament*, Vol. II, 509.

25. Ibid., 517.

26. Brown, *Gospel According to John (i–xii)*, 505.

27. Schnackenburg, *Gospel According to St. John, Volume One*, 155.

28. Smith, *Theology of the Gospel of John*, 149.

29. Morris, *Gospel According to John*, 39–40.

These are a few examples that illustrate the importance of the life theme among some Old Testament and Johannine scholars. Space does not permit further treatment at this time, but more attention will be given to this subject in a subsequent chapter. For the moment, my purpose is simply to illustrate that a strong case can be made for placing a premium value on the theme of life in the Bible. One may agree, however, that the life theme is important in the Bible, yet question whether it could serve as the Bible's central organizing principle. Some persons believe that it is inappropriate to even look for a central organizing principle of the Bible.[30] Others may find such a search to be appropriate but would choose some other theme, such as covenant, promise, or redemption. I will not attempt to address all the permutations of an objection to the life theme as the central organizing principle of the Bible. It would be helpful, however, to deal with the life theme in relation to the kingdom, and proceed from there.

In chapter 1, in my discussion concerning the evangelistic visions of William Abraham and Scott Jones, I offered examples of how we could link kingdom-based evangelistic visions with a life-based evangelistic vision. I would now like to introduce a related yet different concept for you to consider: that we frame the relationship between life and kingdom in reference to ultimate goal or purpose, as distinct from the instruments or means that lead to that ultimate goal or purpose. In this context, the kingdom of God could symbolically serve as an instrument of God's desire (goal) to bring restoration of life to God's human creatures (and all of creation).

It is helpful to analyze kingship in the Ancient Near East (hereafter referred to as ANE) and ancient Israel, for kingship bears a direct relationship to kingdom. It is worth asking: What role does kingship serve? What are kings supposed to accomplish?

There is widespread agreement among scholars that in the ANE, at least until the first millennium BC, kings (in a political sense) were to provide a secure and just environment for the enjoyment of prosperous well-being. In conjunction with this, in a religious sense, they were to mediate the

---

30. Some scholars say that it is impossible to conceive of *an* Old Testament theology or *a* New Testament theology, much less *a* biblical theology. I do not share this perspective, but neither do I want this project to get overly burdened with this discussion. Thus, I am consistently referring to the biblical *theme* of life, rather than the biblical *theology* of life. For my purposes, it is sufficient to note that the life theme is quite important in the Bible and to attempt to discern the evangelistic implications of a strong emphasis on that theme. For more reading regarding biblical theology, I recommend James Barr's book, *The Concept of Biblical Theology*, and Brevard S. Child's book, *Biblical Theology of the Old and New Testaments*.

blessings of the gods (or God). Thus, for example, Whitelam writes that "it was the king's primary duty to guarantee the true administration of justice," which "also guaranteed prosperity and fertility for the nation as a whole."[31] Lambert agrees, noting that in the three ancient Mesopotamian cultures of Sumer, Babylonia, and Assyria, "rulers ruled by the express authority of the gods, and were expected to create a prosperous, well-governed land."[32]

Some scholars believe that the Israelites shared this positive view of kingship in the ANE and its direct correlation to the well-being of the people. In a study of the priestly role that Israelite kings occasionally fulfilled, Rooke concluded that the king would not assume normal priestly duties related to the sanctuary, but that on occasion it would have been "necessary for him to undertake the mediating, priestly role when national interests were at stake, because he was responsible under Yahweh for the nation's well-being."[33] Whitelam concurs that Israel shared the ANE view of kingship, stating that the Israelite view of kingship was "remarkably consistent" with similar views in the ANE.[34]

Others scholars disagree, however, about the Israelite appreciation for kingship, especially during the first millennium BC. Some suggest that the positive view remained until the time of Jesus (reformulated among Jews primarily in messianic terms), while others suggest that this positive outlook waned dramatically. Some writers, for example, view Deuteronomy as a pivotal example of this diminishing appreciation of kingship. John Baines characterizes the Deuteronomistic tradition as being hostile to kingship,[35] and J. G. McConville suggests that Deuteronomy elevated the role of the Torah (constitutional law) in the life of the people, so that "it provides for a kind of kingship that is radically different from kingship as it is known from ancient Near Eastern custom and practice."[36] Ezekiel is also cited as an anti-kingship document in Israelite tradition. Paul Joyce suggests that with Ezekiel's strong focus on the holy God Yahweh, the mediating function of the monarchy has disappeared ("melted away").[37]

31. Whitelam, *Just King*, 36.

32. Lambert, "Kingship in Ancient Mesopotamia," 55.

33. Rooke, "Kingship as Priesthood," 94.

34. Whitelam, *Just King*, 36.

35. Baines, "Ancient Egyptian Kingship," 46.

36. McConville, "King and Messiah in Deuteronomy and the Deuteronomistic History," 281.

37. Joyce, "King and Messiah in Ezekiel," 337.

Given this divergence of opinion about the positive appreciation of kingship in the Judean world during the time of Jesus, some might suggest that it is difficult to place much stock in the idea of kingship being seen as one of God's instruments to bring about God-intended fullness of life. However, the prevalence of kingdom language in the Gospels demonstrates that Jesus assumed at least some basic level of common understanding among the people regarding kingship. Furthermore, Jesus assumed this understanding to be positive (or at worst, neutral). If kingship was in such a state of disrepute, as some scholars believe, Jesus would not have used that image, nor would he have assumed that people would respond to it in any positive way (as illustrated in the link he makes between the announcement of the kingdom and the call to repentance). The key distinction is that the Judean population may not have valued human kingship as strongly as in the past, but they maintained a high esteem for God's kingship. Thus, Jesus's primary goal in announcing the kingdom and inviting people to respond to it was not so that they could be counted as citizens of the kingdom for the sake of the king or the kingdom, but for their own sake, because it is through submission to the rule of King Jesus that they would receive new life in him.

I do not intend to devalue the concept of God's reign. There are times when finite languages simply cannot do justice to thoughts involving the infinite God. The reference to kingdom as the instrument and life as the goal is meant to elevate the concept of life for the theory and practice of evangelism; it is not meant to diminish the concept of kingdom. It may be that the two themes could be considered parallel concepts that offer different conceptual images for us to choose from as we develop theological constructs and ministry practices. Perhaps future scholars will develop improved ways to treat both of these vital topics without diminishing either one. It might even be that we could find ways to link the two.

On the other hand, I want to be careful that the attempt to avoid devaluing the kingdom concept does not in turn diminish the clear point that full, vibrant, teeming life is portrayed in the creation narratives as God's original intention for us and God's creation. If, therefore, we think of Jesus's purpose to be restoration of God's original intention, we must view this full, vibrant, teeming life to be what God seeks to give us in Christ.

Furthermore, this proposal of life as the goal need not be limited to how it relates to the kingdom. The Mosaic covenant could be considered in the same way. The purpose of the covenant was not so Yahweh or the Jews could announce that they were in a covenantal relationship. The covenantal relationship was the vehicle through which the people could experience life as God intended. You may recall those powerful words that Moses spoke just prior to his death: "I call heaven and earth to witness against you to-day, that I have set before you life and death, blessing and curse. Therefore choose life, that you and your offspring may live."[38]

Going back further in biblical history, we see that the purpose of the covenant God made with Noah included both preservation of life and a fertile experience of life: "And you, be fruitful and multiply, teem on the earth and multiply in it."[39] The Abrahamic promise and call can be viewed in the same light: "And I will make of you a great nation, and I will bless you and make your name great, so that you will be a blessing. I will bless those who bless you, and him who dishonors you I will curse, and in you all the families of the earth shall be blessed."[40] The goal of the Abrahamic promise was to bring the rich blessing of God-intended life to all the families of the earth.

Again, having a covenant is not God's ultimate purpose for us. Being a citizen of the kingdom is not God's ultimate purpose for us. These kinds of statements could be conceived of as instrumental. Covenant, kingdom, promise, reconciliation, and atonement: these (and many others) are vitally important concepts, but their value lies in what they relate to—vibrant, abundant life.[41] From the perspective of Scripture this emphasis on life as the initial and central intention of God does greater justice to the fact that the biblical tradition begins with creation. What God intended for all of God's creation in the beginning is reflected in the creation narrative(s), with beautiful expressions of teeming life, fertile abundance, and multiplication, all of which God pronounced as good. If creation of and participation in life was God's original intention for creation, then God's intention in Jesus is a restoration and re-creation of that same life: teeming, fertile, abundant, and good.[42] This directly and powerfully impacts the theory and practice of

38. Deut 30:19.

39. Gen 9:7.

40. Gen 12:2–3.

41. I am grateful to Joseph Dongell for helping me more fully grasp the distinction between instrumentality and goal (personal conversation, February 2, 2010).

42. Jurgen Moltmann in *The Source of Life* (30) disagrees with this perspective. He argues that we should not conceive of God's intention to be that of a restoration back to the original situation that existed in creation. Because the resurrection of Jesus is "something completely new in history," we should visualize God's intention to involve something

evangelism, for it helps shape our understandings of what we are offering in our communication of the good news. We are offering the possibility of participation in the fully orbed life that God originally intended in creation. We are communicating the good news that vibrant living is possible now. We are inviting people to follow the way (reign) of Christ in their lives so they can participate with him in all that he intends and desires for us. The shape or contours or ingredients of this life will be more fully developed in subsequent chapters. At this juncture, I simply (yet importantly) want to reaffirm that while the theological foundation for this project rightly begins with considerations concerning Jesus's synoptic emphasis on the kingdom of God, it more rightly ends with an emphasis on God's ultimate goal of full life, which even more rightly provides the starting place for evangelism.

---

that has yet to be created, rather than visualizing a return to the old Eden. I applaud this mindset and see no problem with envisioning a full life that goes even beyond God's original intention in creation. However, because this "new thing" that will be created in God's resurrection future does not yet exist, we find ourselves limited to the biblical portrayals of what *was* created by God in the beginning. It might be possible to develop a theology of life based on portrayals of the new heaven and the new earth in the book of Revelation, but I would not want to do this at the expense of leaving out references to God's original intentions in creation. The creation narratives and various references to creation throughout the Bible are essential ingredients to a biblically based theology of full life in Jesus.

3

Old Testament Exploration of the Life Theme

THE PREMISE OF THIS book is that the biblical theme of life is one of the primary themes of the Bible, and as such, provides a helpful foundation for the theory and practice of evangelism. It is essential, therefore, to explore the life theme from the perspective of biblical studies, which I will do in chapters 3 and 4. Because it is impossible to engage in a comprehensive survey of all the resources available in the field of biblical studies, I will emphasize selected Old Testament scholars in this chapter and selected Johannine scholars in the next.

Klein: Life Is the Goal

Earlier I referred to the 1991 article by Charles Scobie that mentions a 1983 article by Hans Klein in which life (Old Testament) and new life (New Testament) are proposed together as offering a centralizing theme for biblical study. Klein does not view life/new life "as the centre (*Mitte*) of the Old Testament and New Testament respectively but rather as the goal (*Zielpunkt*) which they envisage."[1] This supports my earlier claim concerning the relationship between life and the kingdom of God, in which life may be considered to be the ultimate goal for human beings and creation, with the kingdom viewed as either one of the instruments God chooses to bring that goal to fruition, or as the arena in which God's full-life intentions take place.

In assessing Klein's proposal, Scobie applauds Klein's attempt to use life as the leading idea of the Bible because it acknowledges the strong differences between the Old and New Testaments, while at the same time

1. Scobie, "Structure of Biblical Theology," 177.

highlights that "all areas of life belong to life under God."[2] One may appreciate Scobie's recognition (through Klein) concerning all of life belonging to God. This is one of the reasons that a strong emphasis on the biblical theme of life provides a significant foundation for evangelism. Even for persons who prefer not to view life as the principle theme of the Bible, a strong emphasis on that theme reminds us that evangelism begins with God's intention to create, bear, and nurture life. Evangelism is intrinsically connected not only to God's creation, but also to God's creative intent. This is a point that merits serious consideration in evangelistic theory and practice.

It Starts with the Living God, and We Are Included

Otto Baab emphasizes that "perhaps the most typical word for identifying the God of the Old Testament is the word 'living.'"[3] As the living God, God acts in history, displays power, and delivers. Of special importance is how the Old Testament characterizes all other gods (idols) in comparison to the living God. Other gods are lifeless, dead, weak, and inadequate.[4] Only the living God, Yahweh, could help, save, and deliver, and only Yahweh had helped, saved, and delivered. Based on their personal experience with the living God, therefore, the Old Testament writers conceived of God as being active in history and active in their personal and corporate lives. Baab writes that "since God is a living God, he is unavoidably involved in all of the complexities and uncertainties of life. His life interacts with that of his people."[5]

Edmond Jacob also places a strong emphasis on the theme of God as a living God. Previously we noted Jacob's contention that "the idea of eternity is secondary to that of life. God is not living because he is eternal, but he is eternal because he is living."[6] Jacob expands on this idea by stating that

2. Scobie, "Structure of Biblical Theology," 177.

3. Baab, *Theology of the Old Testament*, 24.

4. For example, Habakkuk writes, "What profit is an idol when its maker has shaped it, a metal image, a teacher of lies? For its maker trusts in his own creation when he makes speechless idols! Woe to him who says to a wooden thing, Awake; to a silent stone, Arise! Can this teach? Behold, it is overlaid with gold and silver, and there is no breath at all in it" (Hab 2:18–19).

5. Baab, *Theology of the Old Testament*, 26.

6. Jacob, *Theology of the Old Testament*, 38.

"life is what differentiates Yahweh from other gods."[7] Moreover, he shares Baab's perspective that there is a strong link between God's "living-ness" and God's interactions with humanity. "Just as life is a mysterious reality which can only be recognized, so God is a power which imposes itself on man [sic] and comes to meet him [sic] without his being always prepared for it."[8]

Even more significant is Jacob's further contention that not only does God meet us in an imposing way, but the nature of this meeting also includes an invitation to choose life for ourselves, as highlighted by Deuteronomy 30:19. It is only by virtue of making this choice "that man [sic] truly becomes what he is."[9] This concept is helpful because it not only stresses the importance of the theme of life for those who relate with Yahweh, but it also speaks to the nature of what humanity is invited to. We are invited to life, and the one who issues that invitation is the living God who created life, sustains life, and redeems life. We should give this invitation to life a valuable place in evangelistic theory and practice.

The Living God Interacts with Us Relationally

Also germane to this project is the perspective that Jacob and Baab share concerning the relational nature of God's interactions with humanity. Based on a study of God's interactions with Moses at the burning bush, Jacob suggests that one of the important concepts regarding the name of God is that when the Israelites said the name of God, it was God's presence that was emphasized, not God's eternity. Thus, "God is he who is *with* someone."[10]

This perception that relationship with God is inherent in the Israelite understanding of God as the living God is further underscored in Jacob's section on life as the destiny of humanity. He stresses that although God has created human beings as independent persons, humanity "only attains that independence by ever-renewed contact with the one who is the source of his life and the source of all life."[11]

Baab speaks to this point too. In a discussion of the implications of viewing God as Creator, he remarks that "man [sic] and the universe are

7. Jacob, *Theology of the Old Testament*, 39.
8. Ibid., 38.
9. Ibid., 180.
10. Ibid., 52.
11. Ibid., 177.

contingent upon the fact of God. They derive their existence from him and are consequently not self-sufficient or self-contained. They have meaning and value . . . only in the light of their relation to him."[12] Thus, we cannot conceive of the life God intends for us without also conceiving of God relating with us, participating in our lives.

Walther Eichrodt shares similar convictions. He notes a growing awareness throughout Old Testament history of this relational dynamic and suggests that it reached its zenith with the prophets. Based on a sharp focus on the personal nature of God's holiness, the overriding concern for the Israelite people became the question of how they stood in the sight of their holy, sovereign, and covenant-making God.[13] The prophets helped shape a move toward a more individual (not individualistic) understanding of the need to make decisions regarding obedient participation in God's ways in the world. A distinction was made, therefore, between persons who were Israelite by birth and persons who were considered to be a part of God's people through virtue of their individual decisions to obey and follow God.[14] Eichrodt concludes by saying that "what raised the individual divine-human relationship to a new plane, making it a full and living reality, was the way in which the prophets carried to its logical conclusion the belief that man's [sic] relations with God were explicitly personal in character."[15]

This Receiving of Life from God Involves Obedience

It becomes quickly obvious to any reader of the Old Testament that God's granting of life is directly linked to obedience. This is how an integral relationship with the God of life is maintained. Moses's well-known exhortation in Deuteronomy 30, "therefore choose life, that you and your offspring may live," is immediately followed with "loving the LORD your God, obeying his voice and holding fast to him."[16] Earlier in Israel's history, in Exodus 23, God directly links obedience to God's command concerning idolatry, promising to bless their bread and water, remove sickness from among them, prevent barrenness or miscarriage among the women, go

12. Baab, *Theology of the Old Testament*, 47.

13. Eichrodt, *Theology of the Old Testament*, Vol. I, 276.

14. Ibid., 353–8.

15. Ibid., 357.

16. Deut 30:19–20.

before them to drive out their enemies, and grant them God's intended length of life for them.[17] These are just two of many possible examples that illustrate the direct connection between the obedience of God's people and the experience of full life as God intended it for them.

Michael Brown helpfully notes that more is envisioned here than simply receiving the health benefits of the "hygienic practices legislated in the Torah," for " . . . the text indicates that covenantal obedience would bring about supernatural blessings of health—i.e., more than just reaping the rewards of 'clean,' godly living."[18]

Norman Whybray echoes this sentiment in his treatment of the Old Testament conceptions of "the good life." After a chapter-long survey of Exodus through Numbers, he concludes that "these books, while celebrating Yahweh's power and his desire for his people's welfare, will have served as a warning to later generations that the good life is attainable only by faithful obedience to his laws."[19] This is a theme we will return to in the section on insights from the Gospel of John. Before proceeding further, however, it would be prudent to discern how the Old Testament authors conceive of life.

The Concept of Life in the Old Testament

It will be helpful to focus on what the Hebrew people envisioned during the periods when they conceived of life as something they could experience during their earthly lifetime. As has already been seen in the earlier references to Exodus 23 and Deuteronomy 30, the Israelites, if they remained faithful to God's covenant, pictured themselves receiving physical sustenance (blessing of bread and water, Exod 23:25), physical health (removal of sickness, Exod 23:25), reproductive fertility (no miscarriages or barrenness, Exod 23:26; abundantly prosperous in the fruit of their wombs, Deut 30:9), long life (fulfillment of the number of days, Exod 23:26), victory over enemies (Exod 23:27–28, Deut 30:7), success and prosperity with crops and livestock (Deut 30:9), security in the land (Deut 30:16), and compassion (Deut 30:3).

17. Exod 23:20–33.

18. Brown, *Israel's Divine Healer*, 76–77. The "text" to which Brown is referring is Exod 15:26, but in a parenthetical comment he refers to the "related Torah promises" in Exod 23, Lev 26, and Deut 7 and 28.

19. Whybray, *Good Life in the Old Testament*, 41.

Many Old Testament passages refer to the tangible experience of God's intended life. Psalm 84:11b says that " . . . no good thing does he withhold from those who walk uprightly."[20] Psalm 23 refers to green pastures, still waters, an overflowing cup, continual goodness and mercy, and "not wanting" (lacking). Psalm 107 recounts the Lord's wondrous deeds among the redeemed, including deliverance from trouble (verses 6, 13, 19, 20, and 28), a city to dwell in (verses 7 and 36), healing (verse 20), plentiful water (verse 35), and a fruitful yield with crops and livestock (verses 37–38).

Concerning prosperity, Proverbs exhibits a judgmental attitude to the unjust use of riches, but not toward riches in and of themselves. "Honor the Lord with your wealth and with the first fruits of all your produce; then your barns will be filled with plenty, and your vats will be bursting with wine."[21] Proverbs also contends that the search for wisdom and understanding is far more important than the search for gold and jewels, but this does not mean that tangible blessings are contrary to wisdom's desire. To the contrary, "long life is in her right hand; in her left hand are riches and honor. Her ways are ways of pleasantness, and all her paths are peace. She is a tree of life to those who lay hold of her; those who hold her fast are called blessed."[22]

I could share other Old Testament passages to demonstrate the very tangible ways the Hebrew people conceived of life, but these suffice to make the point. These concrete notions concerning what life actually is are fairly strongly agreed upon by a variety of Old Testament scholars. Michael Brown, for example, suggests that Mediterranean peoples shared the idea that God (or whichever deity a people worshipped) would grant blessing to "soil, body, and womb." Thus, the Hebrew people conceived of life as "adequate food supply, health, longevity, and the ability to reproduce."[23] Sister Marie de Lourdes, in commenting on the Hebrew word *hayyim* (life), writes that "for the Hebrew, existence was not sufficient for life. To live meant to be vibrantly happy, to have good health, to be considerably successful in undertakings."[24] Levenson proposes that the Hebrew Bible's concept of life includes " . . . power, skill, confidence, health, blessing, luck, and joy."[25] In

20. Ps 84:11b.
21. Prov 3:9–10.
22. Prov 3:16–18.
23. Brown, *Israel's Divine Healer*, 70.
24. de Lourdes, "Wellsprings of Life," 1825–32.
25. Levenson, *Papers of the Henry Luce III Fellows in Theology*, 142.

his discussion of the Hebrew word *barak* (to bless), Oswalt mentions the concepts of long life, fertile reproduction, prosperity, and success, and goes on to say that the primary role of blessing " . . . seems to have been to confer abundant and effective life upon something . . . or someone . . . "[26]

Norman Whybray engaged in an extensive survey of parts of the Old Testament in an attempt to detect the Old Testament's conception of "the good life." As a result of this survey, he identified twelve features that appear to be prominent: security, a land to live in, power, food, long life, wealth, family, justice, laws, wisdom, pleasure, and trust in God.[27] Notice in Whybray's list that there is a mixture of tangible features such as food and wealth, and intangible features (though no less real) such as power, justice, wisdom, pleasure, and trust in God. This leads into the next section, which considers a related insight by scholars concerning a shift that took place in Israelite conceptions of life.

The Correlation between Life as "Knowing God" and Life as "Receiving God's Gifts"

Jacob and Eichrodt discuss how the Old Testament develops a distinction between the singular blessing of being in fellowship with God as independent from the other blessings that God's people may experience in this life. Jacob talks about the relationship between blessing and the experience of shalom. As the creator and giver of life, blessing originates with God. It is a gift. The result of blessing in the life of the Israelite believer is shalom, "which suggests the idea of abundance, prosperity and peace; this state will only be fully attained in the last times, but for the righteous it can be a present reality, so true is it that there is nothing hoped for which cannot be translated immediately into actual life."[28]

Jacob goes on to comment, however, that there was a shift in Israelite attitudes. Over time they moved to a declining emphasis on earthly abundance and success as the central aspects of the blessed life to a stronger emphasis on relationship with God. This "led to a view of life as no more the possession of God's gifts but of God himself."[29]

26. Oswalt, *Theological Wordbook of the Old Testament*, 132.
27. Whybray, *Good Life in the Old Testament*, 6.
28. Jacob, *Theology of the Old Testament*, 180.
29. Ibid.

Eichrodt observes that this trend was especially powerful in exilic and post-exilic periods. The Hebrew people had experienced horrendous loss during these times, so that their previous vision of what it meant to be blessed by God underwent significant change.[30] They were no longer members of a prosperous nation that seemed to be enjoying God's favor. Their world had been turned upside down. Thus, "in a situation where the individual was struggling for certainty about what the goal of his conduct should be, without having the life and prosperity of his nation to guarantee that his efforts were being successful, and where at the same time the external pressures which burdened the life of the community made a return to a naïve interrelation of blessing and assurance of God impossible, men [sic] readily accepted the prophetic proclamation of fellowship with God as the supreme good."[31] I suggest that this declining stress on "God's gifts" (Jacob) or "natural goods" (Eichrodt), along with an increasing stress on "God himself" (Jacob) or "the religious good of salvation"[32] (Eichrodt), has also found its way into current Christian understanding, and this is quite relevant to the ministry of evangelism.

A relationship with God through Jesus Christ is an essential (and probably *the* essential) dimension of what it means to be a Christ-follower. In this context, then, some Christians choose to downplay the daily blessings of God in life, and also, therefore, in evangelism. This can inadvertently lead to an understanding of the gospel that focuses primarily on an internal relationship with God and ignores the other dimensions of what full life in Christ should and could mean for Christ's followers. God's intentions would be better served, however, if both dynamics were included in gospel understandings and gospel invitations. Yes, first and foremost, we can and should be "in possession of God," but we can also be in "possession of God's gifts" (to use Jacob's words). Why must we divorce the two? Is it really possible to divorce the two? Are not God's gifts of peace, joy, provision,

---

30. Levenson, in "The Fact of Death and the Promise of Life in Israelite Religion" makes a related observation. He notes that earlier in Israelite history the tension between God's promise of life and the fact of death was somewhat (though not completely) resolved by the "semantic range" of the Hebrew Bible's concept of life, so that "when ancient Israelite texts speak of 'life,' they usually mean not deathlessness, but a healthy, blessed existence" (139–54). In post-exilic times, however, due to the traumatic events the people had experienced, a new model began to appear, that of a future resurrection of the dead.

31. Eichrodt, *Theology of the Old Testament*, Vol. II, 360.

32. Ibid.

happiness, reconciliation, service, significance, worship, and more, included in a "package deal" when we are in relationship with God? Can we not invite persons to be in relationship with God and at the same time inform them that this relationship will include God's blessings? Certainly, we must be careful how we communicate the interrelationship between personally relating with God and experiencing God's "other" blessings. We do not want to convey a tit-for-tat invitation, such that persons only enter into relationship with God in order to receive God's abundant blessings. The interface between being in relationship with God and receiving God's blessings is more holistic and integrated than that.

Viewed from the other side of the coin, however, this is precisely the point. Just as we do not want persons to seek God's gifts without seeking God himself, neither do we want them to seek God himself without also seeking God's gifts. If the interface is holistic and integrated, it must be seen as such from each dimension.

Claus Westermann's perspective is useful at this point. In *Blessing in the Bible and the Life of the Church*, he makes a careful distinction between God's deliverance and God's blessing. Deliverance describes the saving acts or events of God, while blessing describes the working of God in the processes of history to bring about fullness of life in daily experience.[33]

In a different work (*What Does the Old Testament Say About God?*), Westermann offers a keen observation concerning the relationship of humanity's creation to this notion of God's working within the processes of history. He suggests that the tendency in Christian theology is to conceive of a disconnect between human creation and the rest of creation, and that this conception is quite unfaithful to the biblical material concerning creation. Human existence is inextricably tied to "living-space (the garden), the provision of food (the trees of the garden), work (the commission to cultivate and preserve), and in particular the community ('a helper fit for him' Gen. 2:18)," so that people "are only human *in* these relations, not beyond them in an abstract existence." In the context of this theological anthropology (or anthropological theology), we can more fully grasp the

33. Westermann, *Blessing in the Bible and the Life of the Church*, 11–14. Elmer Martens in *God's Design* (3–13) also makes a distinction between deliverance and other dimensions of God's intentions with his suggestion that God's fourfold design is clearly outlined in Exod 5:22–6:8 and offers the framework for understanding the Old Testament (and indeed much of the material in the New Testament). This design includes the four components of deliverance, community, relationship, and an enjoyment of the good life.

importance of understanding the role of blessing in Christian life and understanding. "It is the working of the blessing that allows all these necessary parts of human existence to persist: God's blessing allows humanity's food to grow and prosper, preserves human living-space, gives people success in their work, and grants peace (*shalom*) within the community."[34] Blessing for Westermann, therefore, is an ongoing experience.

In a discussion of what salvation means in the Old Testament, Baab notes the integral link between having a relationship with God and the experience of God's blessings. "By tentatively defining salvation as the good which comes to men [sic] in their life with God, we are able to avoid the artificial separation between processes and their consequences, which underlies the general misunderstanding of the Old Testament as reflecting a religion primarily of concrete rewards for good conduct."[35] Eichrodt shares a related insightful viewpoint. He notes that though the exilic and post-exilic prophetic posture helped shape the theological conviction that fellowship with God was the supreme good, the priestly interpretation of the covenant relationship was "characterized by the organic synthesis of earthly blessing and the supreme gift of salvation."[36] He further contends that these two perspectives were "impossible to unite in fruitful tension,"[37] resulting in either a strong focus on fellowship with God as the most valuable consequence of God's salvation, or on natural goods as the most valuable consequence of it.

Despite the difficulty in maintaining a fruitful tension, I encourage us to put forth the effort to move toward an organic synthesis, both in theology and in evangelism. Let us not cast away God's blessing(s) too quickly. God is the creator and giver of life. It was God's original intention in creation for humanity and all of creation to experience fertile life, and this continues to be God's intention. As John Oswalt says, "God gives life. Neither god, nor man, nor rite can do so. Nor does God have to be cajoled to give his blessing. He wishes to give it to all who will trust him (Gen. 12:3)."[38] Let us not downplay God's intentions for us. Let us include God's blessings in our evangelistic vision, communication, and invitation.

---

34. Westermann, *What Does the Old Testament Say About God?*, 41–42.

35. Baab, *Theology of the Old Testament*, 119.

36. Eichrodt, *Theology of the Old Testament*, Vol. II, 363.

37. Ibid.

38. Oswalt, *Theological Wordbook of the Old Testament*, Vol. 1, x285.

Two Tensions or Continuums Are Clearly Present

Before shifting to chapter 4, which discusses insights from John's Gospel, it would be helpful to note that two tensions or continuums clearly emerge from these Old Testament insights. The first is the tension or continuum between conceiving of life in terms of God's tangible blessings versus conceiving of life as the overall or general blessing of knowing God. Hopefully, the importance of addressing this issue was made obvious in the previous section. I will return to this theme in the context of Johannine perspectives on life.

The second tension or continuum is that which Jon Levenson noted between God's promise of life and the clearly observable fact of death, and the post-exilic development of a concept of the resurrection of the dead to address this situation. This is quite similar to the already/not-yet tension related to the kingdom of God that was discussed in chapter 2. I do not wish to revisit that discussion. However, I would like to note that the post-exilic development of the resurrection concept resulted in the postponement of the expectation for earthly benefits related to the life that God would share with God's people. In this context, I want to share pertinent findings from my field research concerning the this-life benefits of following Christ and the after-life benefits of following Christ.

"Why did you decide to follow Jesus?" is the question that I wish to focus on related to this issue. From the 97 interviewees who responded to this question, a total of 113 responses were recorded (some respondents gave more than one reason for deciding to follow Jesus). Of these 113 responses, 8 of them made specific reference to following Jesus because of the result this would have on their life after death (expressed either as fear of hell, desire for heaven, or desire for eternal life). Conversely, 50 responses related directly to some form or measure of improvement in this life. These responses included comments such as "there was a void," "provided the missing piece," "I wanted security," "for protection," "desire to be loved," and "I needed a change in life."

Several references were made to this-life benefits of security, peace, direction, purpose, and hope. These responses were spread fairly evenly throughout all three groups that were asked this question (staff, recent converts, and evangelistically gifted leaders), so that no strongly discernible trend could be seen among the groups. They all expressed a strong interest in (or influence of) this-life benefits as motivating factors in their decision to follow Jesus. In terms of percentages, however, the recent converts leaned somewhat more heavily in this direction. Recent converts represented 33 percent of the total respondents to this question, but in terms of specific references to this-life benefits such as security, peace, purpose, and so on, they accounted for 44 percent of those references. I would not consider this a significant difference, but it does teach us the value of being aware of how profoundly motivating this-life benefits may be for people who have not yet chosen to follow Jesus.

The remaining 55 responses ranged across a wide spectrum, and some of these could also be considered as references to this-life benefits of following Jesus. Responses included "something to believe in," "someone to trust," "I needed him," and "it just made sense." To avoid allowing my pro-life bias to overly influence my interpretation of these responses, I did not include them in the statistical analysis offered in the previous paragraph. However, if one were to add these types of responses to the total number of this-life references, the final number of this-life references would be 75, compared to 8 references to the after-life.[39] Obviously, this is a huge differential. Of the 113 total responses, the 75 this-life responses represent 66 percent, whereas the 8 after-life responses represent only 7 percent.

A valuable insight from the analysis of these responses, therefore, is that we would be wise to pay close attention to the ratio of this-life references versus next-life references in our evangelistic ministry. If most non-Christians are seeking peace, joy, meaning, purpose, sense-making, love, fulfillment, security, and so on in this life, and we focus primarily on "getting right with God" so they can prepare themselves for the after-life, we are communicating with non-Christians in what essentially amounts to a foreign language.

39. The additional 25 this-life responses consist of the following: four responses regarding following Jesus as "the right things to do," 7 persons stating that "it just made sense," 5 references to "truth" or "teaching" or "belief system," 4 respondents suggesting that "it felt right," 4 viewing their Christ-following decision in terms of "something to believe" or "someone to trust," and 1 person who simply said "I needed Him."

4

The Concept of Life in John's Gospel

Zoe, Aionios, and Psyche

LET'S BEGIN WITH A brief treatment of the three primary Greek words related to life in John's Gospel. *Zoe* is the word most often translated as *life* in John, and *aionios* is the adjective that is translated as *eternal*. Thompson suggests that in the Synoptic Gospels the terms *life* and *eternal life* are used interchangeably with *kingdom of God*. The life referred to in this regard speaks not only of quantity of years, but also of a quality of living that would be consistent with the age to come. This age-to-come life had a strong futuristic orientation in the Synoptics, so that while a person's present life strongly impacts a person's future, for people who responded to Jesus's call the anticipated blessing of eternal life would be primarily experienced in some "future state of blessedness."[1] Thompson believes that in John's Gospel *life* and *eternal life* are also synonymous, and although the phrase *kingdom of God* only appears twice in John, it is used interchangeably with *life* and *eternal life*.

Thompson notes that although many biblical scholars attribute an "age-to-come" character to life and eternal life in John's Gospel, just as in the Synoptics, there are some who would question this. Most notably is Schackenburg, who believes that John's distinction is not between life in this age versus life in the age to come (temporal), but rather life in this earthly realm versus life in the heavenly realm (spatial).[2]

1. Thompson, "Eternal Life in the Gospel of John," 37.
2. Ibid., 38.

Although this contrast is helpful, an even more helpful contrast is that between John's use of *zoe* and his use of *psyche*. *Psyche* in John normally refers to "human life which can be given up" and is most often translated in English as *soul,* although sometimes it is also translated as *life.* Thompson notes that although *psyche* can be given up (such as when Jesus refers to giving up his life for the sheep in John 10), "zoe is life which cannot be taken away, life which is imperishable. Zoe cannot be lost, since it is true, heavenly, God-given life." All human beings have *psyche*, but not all human beings have *zoe*, for *zoe* only comes from God through Jesus.[3]

Leon Morris also deals with John's usage of *zoe* and *psyche*. Regarding *zoe*, he agrees with Thompson that *life* and *eternal life* mean the same thing for John. Concerning *psyche*, Morris shares Thompson's basic sentiments, but he phrases it just a bit differently. Morris refers to *psyche* as "ordinary physical life" and observes that most often John uses this word when he refers to someone giving up or laying down his or her life. He suggests that John 12:25 is a good example of how John uses the two differently, where Jesus says "whoever loves his life (*psyche*) loses it, and whoever hates his life (*psyche*) in this world will keep it for eternal life (*zoe*)."[4]

Clearly John makes an important distinction in the use of *psyche* and *zoe*, but it is difficult to discern with certainty what that distinction is. Does *psyche* refer to life on the earthly plane while *zoe* refers to life on the heavenly plane? Is *zoe* a reference to divine life while *psyche* is a reference to human life? Neither of these questions seems satisfactory because they appear to devalue the "crossing of planes or realms" that Jesus undertook in the incarnation. Thompson is heading in the right direction when she says that all people have *psyche* but not all people have *zoe*, but to state any definitive conclusions beyond this assessment would be unwise.

Despite some uncertainty about the precise Johannine distinctions between *zoe* and *psyche*, one of the commonly shared beliefs among biblical scholars is that John's perception of life has a strong emphasis on its source in God. C. H. Dodd, for example, proposes that the adjective *eternal* is more a qualitative than a quantitative description. It includes a reference to everlastingness, but "its everlastingness is a function of its divine quality," not the other way around.[5] Richard Thomas also emphasizes the relationship of eternal to its source in and connection to God. He writes that "the

3. Thompson, "Eternal Life in the Gospel of John," 38–39.
4. Morris, *Jesus Is the Christ*, 190–1.
5. Dodd, *Interpretation of the Fourth Gospel*, 149.

epithet 'eternal' indicates the divine source and permanent nature of the life that Jesus proclaimed and proffered."[6] Remember that this Johannine connection of life to its source in God was a prominent Old Testament theme as well.

The Relationship of Eternal Life to Knowing God

Knowing God Is Eternal Life

As you study John's Gospel, it becomes quickly apparent that the Old Testament tension or continuum between the blessing of knowing God and the "other" blessings of God's tangible gifts has remained an integral part of the experience of God's followers. Perhaps more than any other Gospel, John makes a strong case for conceiving of life as the gift and experience of knowing God relationally through believing in Jesus and obeying God's word (written and incarnate). In this sense, then, John seems to characterize life not as a commodity that one is given (or awarded) because they choose to believe, know, and obey God. Instead, the very experience itself of believing, knowing, and obeying God *is* life. John lays the foundation for this perspective from the beginning of his Gospel by noting the direct connection between God, the Word, creation, and life. "In the beginning was the Word, and the Word was with God, and the Word was God. He was in the beginning with God. All things were made through him, and without him was not any thing made that was made. In him was life, and the life was the light of men."[7]

In chapter 3, I mentioned the strong Old Testament assertion that God is the living God, and is, therefore, the source of all life. As the incarnate Word who shared in the creation of life and all that exists, and as the one who has been granted by the Father to have life in himself (see John 5:26), Jesus is the source of life for those who believe in him and, therefore, have experiential knowledge of God. In Jesus's prayer recorded in John 17, he said, "Father, the hour has come; glorify your Son that the Son may glorify you, since you have given him authority over all flesh, to give eternal life to all whom you have given him. And this is eternal life, that they know you

---

6. Thomas, "The Meaning of the Terms 'Life' and 'Death,'" 204.

7. John 1:1–4.

the only true God, and Jesus Christ whom you have sent."[8] Jesus says very plainly here that to know God is eternal life.

Thompson agrees with this perspective, asserting that "only those who know God, who live in fellowship with God and in harmony with the purposes of God, have eternal life, not because living in fellowship with God merits eternal life as a reward, but because fellowship with God is already to have a share in God's own life."[9] Many share Thompson's view. Leon Morris writes that "the knowledge of God and of Christ is itself eternal life. It is not that it brings eternal life: it is itself that life."[10] I made earlier mention of John laying the foundation for this perception in the early verses of his Gospel. Koester roots his viewpoint in John's prologue too, observing that the theme of God as Creator and giver of life is very basic to John's theology, and that the early mention of life, creation, and light indicates that if human beings "are to live they must receive life from God. This means that in John's Gospel, life is understood relationally. To have life is to relate to the God who is the source of all life . . . To have true life is to know and trust God and his Word."[11] C. K. Barrett agrees, noting that the relationship that Jesus has with the Father involves "love, obedience, and mutual indwelling," and that when a person knows God through Jesus, a comparable relationship develops. Furthermore, this knowing "of God and Christ confers, or rather is, eternal life."[12]

We can readily see the strong argument that can be made from John's Gospel to conceive of life more in terms of the general blessing of knowing God than in terms of the more tangible and specific blessings God grants us. This line of reasoning is strengthened even further when one explores the relationship between believing, knowing, and obeying God, along with the closely linked idea of abiding. Though scholars will not agree about every detail and nuance of this discussion, there is a generally agreed-upon perspective that John's Gospel portrays life in Christ as an ongoing relationship with God through Jesus that begins with believing (trusting, following, surrendering to), which results in knowing (experiential, relational knowledge), and is continuously sustained through obeying (the incarnate Word and the written word, through the guidance of the Spirit) and abiding (staying connected to Jesus and bearing fruit in community with other believers).

8. John 17:1–3.

9. Thompson, *Eternal Life*, 40.

10. Morris, *Jesus Is the Christ*, 204.

11. Koester, *Word of Life*, 31–32.

12. Barrett, *Gospel According to St. John*, 136.

Believing, Knowing, Obeying, and Abiding

Believing

This ongoing relationship, from the human perspective, begins with be-lieving. Leon Morris tells us that the verb *to believe* is used ninety-eight times in John's Gospel, far more than in any other New Testament book, while the noun for *faith* is not used at all.[13] Morris summarizes John's use of the verb under four headings. The *simple dative* "conveys the idea of giv-ing credence to someone or something, of accepting a statement as true." *Believing that* (with the Greek word *hoti*) underscores that "believing" has specific content, so that John's reader is not invited simply to believe in a non-directed, general sense, but rather to believe specifically in Jesus. *Believing "in" or "on"* (often with the Greek preposition *eis*, which signi-fies *into*) indicates not only that Jesus is the intended target or content of believing, but also that believing has more to do with personal trust than with acknowledgement of factual veracity. Finally, the *absolute use* stresses the essential relationship between believing and experiencing real life. Life is made available through Jesus, but only if the person believes. "There is nothing we can bring to the quest for life; it comes as God's good gift. All that we do is receive it trustingly." Morris goes on to suggest that one should not overemphasize the specific differences of John's four uses of *believe*, but rather should see the basic unity present among them all, so that the gen-eral point is that through believing in Jesus, God's Son, people receive the life that he came to bring.[14]

F. F. Bruce suggests that "faith involved both believing in and believ-ing that: believing in Jesus is emphasized as the way of life through the gospel, but believing in him implies certain things about him—that he is 'the Christ, the Son of God.'"[15] Bruce later refers to *believing in* as "personal faith" and *believing that* as "propositional faith,"[16] which is somewhat simi-lar to Morris's contention that believing must have content.

Perhaps more closely related to Morris's understanding, however, is Bruce's proposal that believing in Jesus involves "total self-commitment" to

13. Morris, *Jesus Is the Christ*, 170.
14. Ibid., 170–89.
15. Bruce, *Gospel of John*, 12.
16. Ibid., 395.

him.[17] George Mlakuzhyll has studied the Gospel of John from an Indian perspective as influenced by Hindu religious tradition. He notes that in the Hindu tradition three paths of salvation are offered: works, knowledge, and loving devotion. He suggests that John's Gospel emphasizes the path of faith and love, which results in the believer experiencing a relational knowledge of God that transforms the person's life and leads them to be an instrument of God's love for others.[18] Of particular interest to our discussion of what *believing* means in John's Gospel, Mlakuzhyll proposes that one of the primary features of faith in John's Gospel is that a person becomes a believer through welcoming the Word of God, and that "it is not enough to welcome the Word of God once and for all, but one must constantly be under the influence of the Word of God to continue to be a child of God . . . this continuity of personal commitment is implied by the present participial phrase 'those believing in his name' (1,12; see also 'believing' at 20,31)."[19] Morris concurs with this viewpoint. In commenting on Jesus's words in John 6:29 ("This is the work of God, that you believe in him whom he has sent"), he says that "the present tense here denotes continuing attitude, not the once-for-all decision."[20]

Morris, Bruce, and Mlakuzhyll are just three of many scholars who emphasize the ongoing nature of *believing* in John's Gospel. It is obvious, therefore, that John conceives of believing as a lifelong relationship of trusting in Jesus and following his ways, as opposed to a one-time faith transaction that has little or no impact on the rest of a person's life.

Knowing and Obeying

We can quickly recognize, therefore, that believing is part of a lifelong process that includes knowing God and obeying God. In order to discuss the truths involved, we must necessarily speak of them as separate and distinct entities, but believing, knowing, and obeying are very closely connected. As a person enters into the lifelong relationship of trusting Jesus and following

17. Bruce, *Gospel of John*, 153.

18. Mklakuzhll (*Abundant Life*, 8) writes that "the Beloved Disciple invites the readers to a life of faith and love, a faith in Jesus Christ that grows into an experiential knowledge of him and ensues in Christlike love, a love that is enlivened by a dynamic faith and enlightened by an intimate knowledge, a life that is transformed by faith in and knowledge of Jesus Christ, a '*Christic*' life (life that flows from Christ) flowering into mutual love."

19. Mlakuzhyll, *Abundant Life*, 23–24.

20. Morris, *Gospel According to John*, 360.

his ways, that person, therefore, also begins the process of knowing God (through Jesus) relationally, and the following of God's ways clearly implies a level of obedience. The themes of obeying God and relating with God personally were dealt with in chapter 3, and they are certainly no less important in John's Gospel. It is crucial to John's conception of life in Christ that believers actually know God in a personal, relational, and intimate manner, and that this experiential knowledge results in obedience to God's ways. D. Moody Smith agrees with this idea, but he also observes that we should avoid thinking of knowing God as subsequent to believing God. Smith proposes that knowing God is not "a step beyond believing, but the correlate of believing. Such knowledge can never be divorced from faith or be played off against faith, for it belongs to the very nature of faith in Jesus Christ to know the one who is believed and trusted."[21] This notion of "correlatedness" helps us more fully grasp the strong interconnectedness between believing, knowing, and obeying God.[22] Smith, in fact, follows up his comments about faith and knowledge with thoughts related to obedience. In a section of his book dealing with Jesus and the community of believers, he writes that "believing obedience is the essence of discipleship and the church."[23] Bruce echoes this concept, noting that "there is no true faith without obedience, no true obedience without faith."[24] Just as our believing in Jesus does not occur in a vacuum, neither is our lifelong relationship of believing (trusting and following) disconnected from our knowing and obeying God.

Abiding

Abiding is a concept very closely related to this discussion. Raymond Brown's treatment of the relationship between abiding and ecclesiology is helpful in this regard. Brown maintains that the vine and branches imagery in John 15, taken along with the sheep and shepherd imagery in chapter 10, help us understand that "the core of ecclesiology is a personal, ongoing relation to the life-giver come down from God," so that "it is all important for

21. Smith, *Theology of the Gospel of John*, 97.

22. In a corollary fashion, John Oswalt (*On Being a Christian*, 79–86) highlights "the interdependence of belief and love and obedience" in 1 John 5:1–5, and uses the phrase "delighted obedience" to refer to the character of our obedience to the One whom we trust and know.

23. Smith, *Theology of the Gospel of John*, 138.

24. Bruce, *Gospel of John*, 160.

each person not only to believe in Jesus but to remain attached to him, for he continues as an active life-giver and life-nourisher in the community."[25]

Additionally, F. F. Bruce contends that the language of Jesus in John 6:56 ("whoever feeds on my flesh and drinks my blood abides in me, and I in him") "denotes that faith-union by which a mutual indwelling, a 'co-inherence' of Jesus and his people is established."[26] Leon Morris shares a similar perspective concerning John 6, writing that the person "who eats and drinks 'abideth' (the tense is continuous; it denotes more than a reflecting contact) in Christ."[27]

Believing, Knowing, Obeying, and Abiding: Hearing Directly from John

What does John say about believing, knowing, obeying, and abiding? In one example, he writes of the light (which most scholars take to mean Jesus the incarnate Word) that "He was in the world, and the world was made through him, yet the world did not know him."[28] It is instructive that in detailing the human situation the incarnate Word was sent to earth to address, John first mentions not unbelief as the primary dilemma, but a lack of knowing God. In chapter 3, John the Baptist says that "whoever believes in the Son has eternal life; whoever does not obey the Son shall not see life, but the wrath of God remains on him."[29] A direct connection is made here between believing and obeying.

In chapter 10, Jesus uses the imagery of the sheep and shepherd to describe (at least in part) what it means to experience life in him. He emphasizes that the shepherd knows the sheep and the sheep know the shepherd. They know the shepherd's voice and will follow him when he calls them in or out of pasture. Furthermore, Jesus links knowing with believing as he continues his discussion with the unbelieving Jewish leaders. "I told you, and you do not believe. The works that I do in my Father's name bear witness about me, but you do not believe because you are not part of my flock. My sheep hear my voice, and I know them, and they follow me."[30] In the Lazarus story, we find Jesus saying to Martha that "everyone who lives

25. Brown, *Churches the Apostles Left Behind*, 87–95.

26. Bruce, *Gospel of John*, 160.

27. Morris, *Gospel According to John*, 380.

28. John 1:10.

29. John 3:36.

30. John 10:25–27.

and believes in me shall never die."[31] Note the grouping together here of *living* and *believing*.

In chapter 15, Jesus is addressing the disciples. He tells them: "As the Father has loved me, so have I loved you. Abide in my love. If you keep my commandments, you will abide in my love, just as I have kept my Father's commandments and abide in his love."[32] Jesus is straightforward in relating obedience (keeping of commandments) with relationship (abiding in his love). These passages from John's Gospel help illustrate John's deep-seated belief that life in Christ involves believing, knowing, obeying, and abiding.

The Relationship of the Johannine Conception of Life in Christ to Believing, Knowing, Obeying, and Abiding

Given this strong emphasis throughout John's Gospel, it is no surprise that some biblical scholars suggest that the Johannine conception of life in Christ focuses primarily on the general blessing of knowing God and pays scant attention to other tangible blessings of God. In a book concerning early Christianity and the Jewish perspective on land, W. D. Davies connects this Johannine perspective to the reformulation that John crafts concerning the "holy spaces" of Judaism. He proposes, for example, that in chapters 8 and 9 of his Gospel, John portrays the replacement of the Jerusalem temple with the temple of Jesus's body. Based especially on Jesus's "I am" claim in 8:58 and his departure from the temple in 8:59, Davies suggests that "we find the implication that, for John, 'I am' has departed from the Temple, that 'holy space' is no longer the abode of the Divine Presence. The Shekinah is no longer *there*, but is now found wherever Christ is."[33]

Davies makes a similar point regarding Jesus's encounter with the Samaritan woman at Jacob's well. In this passage, he sees a contrast being made between the water that Jesus provides and the water that one can draw from Jacob's well, so that the focus is not on contrasting Jesus with Jacob, but on contrasting the holy space of Jacob's well with the new source of living water.

Likewise, in the healing at the pool of Bethesda in John 5, "there is here a replacement of a Jewish holy space, with its holy water, by the living

31. John 11:26a.
32. John 15:9–10.
33. Davies, *Gospel and the Land*, 295.

Word."[34] The strong implication throughout Davies's treatment of John's Gospel is that John centers all his attention on Jesus as the source of life and sustenance, so that if one wishes to speak of life in Christ, one must speak primarily of him and not of any tangible gifts that would be external to him. As Davies says, "what was significant to John was the descent of Jesus from above and his ascent thither. The fundamental spatial symbolism of the Fourth Gospel was not horizontal but vertical."[35]

The idea of focusing our attention on Jesus is certainly laudable, for he is the author, source, and giver of life. There is no question that John invites his readers to believe, know, obey, and abide in Jesus, and that in so doing they will experience the life he came to give. Unfortunately, however, my experience has been that some persons who embrace this strong emphasis on Jesus make a corollary assumption that is erroneous. They assume that one should not speak of knowing Jesus experientially in a personal, trusting, obedient, and abiding relationship and also speak of experiencing tangible blessings from God, such as health, provision, joy, peace, meaning, and significance. Davies, for example, shares important insights regarding the Johannine replacement of Jewish holy spaces (and I would add Jewish holy practices) with the living person of Jesus. However, he goes too far when he ignores the "horizontal" spatial symbolism (to use his words) that is found in John. Consider the incident at the pool of Bethesda. Davies makes a valid point in contrasting the healing that is now found in Jesus with the healing that was previously found at this sacred site, but it's almost as though he forgets that what took place that day was, in fact, a healing. A man had been lame for thirty-eight years, and Jesus made it possible for him to walk again. Certainly in that man's mind his new ability to walk was part of his experience of life in Christ. Similarly, Davies points out the contrast made in John 4 between the water of Jacob's well and the living water of Jesus, and this is a contrast well worth observing. Yet after leaving the region of Samaria and arriving in Galilee, Jesus heals the official's son, and after healing the man at the pool of Bethesda, he feeds the five thousand. Surely the official and his son would have considered the son's healing to be at least one dimension of their experience of life in Christ, as would the five thousand have felt about being fed the loaves and fishes by the seashore. Not only were they fed, but they were fed until all were satisfied, with

34. Davies, *Gospel and the Land*, 309.
35. Ibid., 335.

enough leftovers for each disciple to gather a basketful of food. This is not only provision, but provision in abundance.

We should not downplay the vital importance of knowing God as the central experience of the life Jesus came to bring us. However, neither should we downplay the other tangible gifts that Jesus grants to his followers. Health, provision, peace, joy, purpose, significance, and human relationships—all these and more are included in the life Christ offers us. I am reminded of Jesus's words in Matthew 6 where he encourages his followers not to worry about what they will eat or what they will wear, because if they seek God's kingdom and righteousness, "all these things will be added to you."[36] Jesus invites us to focus on developing our relationship with him, which involves believing, trusting, knowing, obeying, and abiding. This is to be what centers us in the life that he brings. With this we may wholeheartedly agree, and Jesus expresses this in John 6 when he tells the crowd not to "labor for the food that perishes, but for the food that endures to eternal life."[37] In this context, our focus should not be on a selfish seeking after tangible blessings instead of a healthy seeking after relationship with God. However, we may also expect that because of Jesus's great love for us, and because of God's original intention in creation for us to live with health, provision, peace, joy, and significance, we will experience tangible gifts and blessings as part of the process of our lifelong journey with Christ. This is an appropriate biblical portrayal of life in Christ. Furthermore, since this is an appropriate biblical portrayal of the life that Christ invites persons to enter into, it is imperative that we discern ways to include this portrayal in evangelistic theory and practice. I honor the tension that exists here. I understand how difficult it is to focus on knowing God while yet also anticipating God's tangible blessings to be a part of that experience of knowing.

The difficulty of doing this, the tension that this creates for us, is evident among biblical scholars. Philippe Kabongo-Mbaya deals with this tension in his treatment of what John means by *life in abundance* in 10:10. He proposes that we must consider the context of chapters 8 and 9 in interpreting this phrase. Chapter 8 shows Jesus in the temple talking with the Jewish leaders, and chapter 9 shows an unflattering picture of people in the Jewish synagogue following the healing of the blind man. In addition to this immediate context within John's Gospel, Kabongo-Mbaya also suggests that we remember the historical context of the Gospel, which was

36. Matt 6:33b.
37. John 6:27a.

written around 90 AD, and was most likely written by a representative (or representatives) of the Johannine Jewish-Christian sect that had been removed from the synagogue due to their theological stance.[38] The shepherd and sheep imagery in chapter 10, therefore, was the Johannine community's way of "affirming their own status in relation to the rabbinate and other Jewish and Judeo-Christian currents of the time; they were attacking the very foundation of the synagogue's superiority and its claim to be the sole and exclusive place of communion with the God of the Covenant."[39]

In this context, then, "the abundance in question here cannot be reduced simply to an abundance of goods, giving life an unlimited, but one-sided quantitative dimension."[40] Moving out of poverty and having their other troubles (exclusion, loss of identity, and so on) disappear, therefore, is not what the Johannine Christians equated with life in abundance. Rather, it was "in face of these realities and despite them, opposing them and going beyond them that Johannine theology articulates the quality of trust in God—a God who lends our finite lives a fullness of meaning and truth that no extravagance of bread, no orgy by the powers-that-be can give them."[41] It seems at this point, therefore, that Kabongo-Mbaya wants to emphasize the "trust in God" and the consequent "fullness of meaning and truth" over against the "extravagance of bread." If we are truly speaking of an undue extravagance of bread, I would heartily agree, but an extravagance of provision or an orgy of health is not what I'm proposing. Rather, I propose that adequate provision to sustain life on the horizontal sphere is part of God's intention in the life Christ came to bring. The imagery in John 10 lends itself to this proposal too, for the shepherd's job is not simply to keep

38. There is fairly wide agreement among biblical scholars concerning this historical context to John's Gospel. F. F. Bruce (*The Gospel of John*, 13), for example, observes that "the debate between the disciples and the synagogue authorities reached a critical stage around AD 90, when one of the prayers in the synagogue service was reworded so as effectively to exclude the followers of Jesus. It was probably against this background that the Fourth Gospel was published." Similarly, Gerard Sloyan (*John: Interpretation*, 1) notes that "John was the document of a local church that had broken finally with the synagogue." Raymond Brown (*Community of the Beloved Disciple*, 22–23) concurs with this general sentiment, noting that "by the time the gospel was written the Johannine Christians had been expelled from the synagogues," and though "expulsion from the synagogues was now past" the "persecution (16:2–3) continues." He also dates the writing of the gospel at around AD 90.

39. Kabongo-Mbaya, "Life in Abundance," 73.

40. Ibid., 73–74.

41. Ibid., 74.

the sheep safely guarded in the sheepfold at night, but it is also to provide them safe passage to and from the pasture, so that they can find the basic provisions of food and water. Kabongo-Mbaya seems to agree on this point, for at the conclusion of his article, he writes that "abundant life in John 10.10 is a complex and essentially inclusive image. It links the sheepfold and pasture; it guarantees the possibility for the sheep, henceforth to go in and out. Life inside and life outside are held together and reconciled, as are security and freedom."[42] Kabongo-Mbaya struggles with the tension, but in the end he embraces it rather than dissolves it, and this is noteworthy.

V. J. John also embraces the tension. He compares abundant life with "plentiful pasture," and writes that life in its "highest degree" is life "lived in relation to God," which makes it "more meaningful and enriching." While emphasizing life lived in relation to God, though, he also asserts that "life cannot be viewed apart from socio-economic realities and its relation to physical wellbeing," for "while they in themselves are not enough to lead an abundant life, together with them life becomes more meaningful and enriching."[43]

Stephen Smalley suggests that the incarnation helps us understand how God gives of God's self through material things, so that in John the notions of creation and history are taken very seriously. This leads to an appreciation of the sacramental nature of John's writing (which in this context means not an emphasis on particular sacraments, but rather on how "the spirit can give life to matter in a qualitatively new way"), and this in turn teaches us that for John "life in all its aspects—physical as well as spiritual—engaged his attention."[44]

C. F. D. Moule addresses the tension between what Smalley calls "physical" and "spiritual" by reminding us of the general biblical perspective that human beings are indivisible wholes that should not be thought of primarily as consisting of separate component parts such as soul and body. With this foundation, he then addresses the raising of Lazarus and points out that this sign shares with the Johannine signs that precede it "the characteristic that Jesus is portrayed as bestowing something that belongs to the normal, physical life on earth, but bestowing it in an abnormal, a transcendent, manner."[45] In Jesus, therefore, Moule sees a bringing together

---

42. Kabongo-Mbaya, "Life in Abundance," 74.

43. John, "Concept of 'Life,'" 96–97.

44. Smalley, *John*, 207–9.

45. Moule, "Meaning of 'Life,'" 122.

of all "degrees of being," which means that "in this life Christ brings life and food and health and sight," but "if you ask what the bigger life of the age to come looks like, you are told nothing at all except that it means contact with God and Christ, and that such contact is a matter of obedience."[46] Moule is not correct in asserting that we are told nothing at all about the life of the age to come, but this is not the place to address that issue. The more important insight related to the present discussion is his notion that all degrees of being are brought together in Jesus, for this seems to be a helpful image for addressing the tension we have been dealing with.

Ben Witherington, in commenting on Jesus's bread of life conversation in John 6, acknowledges Jesus's admonition in verse 27 that I referenced previously, where Jesus encourages the crowd to seek the food that endures to eternal life. Witherington goes on to add, however, that since Jesus did in fact feed the five thousand, he is not depicting a spitefulness or disdain toward food or other physical things, but "rather that he wishes to use them to point to a food that is more sustaining, crucial, indeed, a food that endures to eternal life." In this sense, therefore, "Jesus is portrayed as being willing to provide both physical and spiritual food, not just the latter."[47]

One dimension of Witherington's interpretational context is his firm belief in the relationship of John's Gospel to the Jewish Wisdom literature. Especially pertinent is his definition of wisdom as "skill in living well, making the right decisions, which prolong and promote life, health, and happiness, even in a dark world."[48] It is obvious that if John is founded in part on a clear relationship to Jewish Wisdom literature, then one cannot ignore this emphasis on living well and enjoying health and happiness in this world. To do so would be to disregard an important dimension of the context of John's Gospel.

In evangelistic theory and practice we should not suggest that persons can get rich by following Jesus, nor should we promise them a long life free of illness. We should, however, with integrity, invite persons to an experience of full life in Jesus Christ that centers on developing a believing, trusting, obeying, abiding relationship with him. Moreover, we should mention that this experience of full life in Jesus will almost certainly include some portion of the tangible benefits of health, provision, joy, peace, significance, and purpose. I say "*almost* certainly include *some* portion of the tangible

46. Ibid., 124.
47. Witherington, *John's Wisdom*, 155.
48. Ibid., 58.

51

benefits" because we are not God and we are unable to know the future for each individual. We do not know why some persons die of cancer and others do not, or why some persons lose their jobs while others do not. We do not know which persons will experience a call from God to a life of poverty working in the slums of Calcutta or which persons will be called to witness to Jesus's grace in the boardrooms of the world. However, we do know that God's intention in Jesus is for us to experience full and vital living that is centered in a personal, obedient relationship with him, but also experienced in the tangible physical world.

Eternal as Future and Present in John's Gospel

In addition to the tension regarding life as the general blessing of knowing God versus life as receiving God's more tangible blessings, we may also query John's Gospel concerning the tension we discovered in our Old Testament work regarding the when of the life that God intends for us. What, therefore, is the general perspective found in John's Gospel concerning the timing of when Christ-followers experience eternal life? The general consensus among biblical scholars is that eternal life for John is consistent with the general perspective of the already and not-yet nature of the kingdom, but perhaps with a stronger leaning toward a present-day orientation. C. H. Dodd probably leans more passionately toward the present-day experience of eternal life than other scholars. Earlier mention was made of Dodd's "placement" of eternal life more fully in the divine quality of that life rather than in its quantitative length. Dodd, in fact, believes this so deeply that he even goes so far as to say that in John eternal life describes "a life which has properly speaking neither past nor future, but is lived in God's eternal To-day."[49] Dodd does not deny the everlasting dimension of eternal life, admitting that at the general resurrection believers will enter into that everlasting dimension, but he believes that this dimension is far less important to John than is the present experience of the divine quality of that life. Therefore, "for John this present enjoyment of eternal life has become the controlling and all important conception."[50]

Leon Morris makes a similar point in his comments concerning Jesus's words to Martha in John 11:25–26.[51] Morris acknowledges the relationship

49. Dodd, *Interpretation of the Fourth Gospel*, 150.

50. Ibid., 149.

51. "I am the resurrection and the life. Whoever believes in me, though he die, yet

of eternal life to the life of the age to come, but he goes on to say that "the moment a man puts his trust in Jesus he begins to experience that life of the age to come which cannot be touched by death. Jesus is bringing Martha a present power, not the promise of a future good."[52]

Other scholars agree with the present-day orientation of John's perspective regarding eternal life, but they also include references to future fulfillment. Barrett, for example, in a discussion of salvation in John's Gospel, observes that a variety of eschatological views were present in the Judaism of Jesus's day, but the general tendency was "to regard salvation as the fruit of a future act of God." Outside Judaism, however, just the opposite was true. "Salvation was a present experience given by God to men [sic], either through sacraments or through knowledge."[53] Barrett suggests that John would naturally have been familiar with both perspectives, and perhaps more importantly, he proposes that John considered that "the old eschatological notion of salvation was not adequate for Christian use, because the promised salvation was now partly fulfilled, and could no longer be described as purely future."[54] This present partial fulfillment of God's intentions for humankind leaves room, therefore, for an understanding that while eternal life is experienced to some degree prior to death, there is yet more to be experienced in a future time after death.

Craig Koester agrees, but he arrives at this perspective a bit differently. He distinguishes between physical life and relational life, noting that while all persons are given physical life from God, not everyone has the relational life from God that comes through believing in God. For the believer, therefore, "eternal life begins now, in faith, and it continues beyond death through the promise of resurrection."[55]

Stephen Smalley bases a comparable perspective on the notion that eternal life (equated with salvation) is "a regular Johannine term for the wholeness which man [sic] needs and can obtain." Because this wholeness comes through the historical "work" of Jesus (incarnation through exaltation), it also begins historically in the present with the believer and involves our past, present, and future. We have been led out of our past darkness

shall he live, and everyone who lives and believes in me shall never die. Do you believe this?"

52. Morris, *Gospel According to John*, 550.
53. Barrett, *Gospel According to St. John*, 65.
54. Ibid., 67.
55. Koester, *The Word of Life*, 32.

into present life and light, and in the present, the risen Christ sustains us. However, "there is a future tense as well. The person who honors the Son of God now is promised the 'resurrection of life' in the age to come."[56]

Raymond Brown approaches this issue by using a vertical versus horizontal framework. He argues that the primary biblical view of salvation is horizontal, because God so often acts within history. A vertical view of salvation focuses more strongly on the existence of an earthly realm and a heavenly realm, so that salvation involves moving from the earthly to the heavenly. Brown suggests that John leans toward a vertical view of salvation. However, there is some of the horizontal view in John too, as evidenced by the strong insistence that "salvation is from the Jews" (4:21–23), by the fact that the Word was made flesh (Jesus lived in a particular body, in a particular time, in a particular place), and by the obviously historical and real experience of the crucifixion, resurrection, and ascension. Thus, Brown says, "the Johannine view of salvation is both vertical and horizontal. The dominant vertical aspect expresses the uniqueness of the divine intervention in Jesus; the horizontal aspect establishes a relationship between this intervention and what has gone before and what follows."[57]

D. Moody Smith addresses the question of when in a quite helpful way. He suggests that the eschatological age overlaps with the present age in such a way that though we know we only experience the eschatological quality of eternal life here on earth in a provisional way, what we do experience in the present is indeed of an eschatological quality. "Because of the presence of life, the believing community also participates in other aspects of the eschatological age, such as joy (Greek: *thara*) and peace (*eirene*). When Jesus says that he has come in order that people may have life and have it more abundantly (10:10) he means life characterized by joy and peace, eschatological life."[58] Moreover, Smith talks about the relationship between the life we experience now and the fact that the everlasting nature of eternal life does include victory over physical death. There is a symbiotic relationship between the two. Believers know that they will experience life with God after physical death here on earth, and this knowledge impacts their present experience of eschatological life because it frees them from worry about what will happen to them after they die. They are, therefore, able to more fully invest themselves in believing, knowing, obeying, and

56. Smalley, *John*, 203–4.
57. Brown, *Introduction to the Gospel of John*, 235–7.
58. Smith, *Theology of the Gospel of John*, 150.

abiding in Jesus. In this context, therefore, "the possession or gift of eternal life in the believer's present existence is integrally related to the assurance of its permanence."[59] Witherington concurs: "At some point faith must win out over fear in the believer's life, and then she or he becomes free to live and to die without undue concern about the 'valley of the shadow', free to risk his or her life for the sake of Christ."[60]

John's Perspective on Human and Divine Involvement in Our Entry into Life

To this point we have discussed the notion of life in John's Gospel from the perspective of various tensions or continuums that are apparent there, including that between life as knowing God versus life as receiving God's more tangible blessings and that between life as something we experience now versus something we primarily experience after death. Another possible tension or continuum exists concerning how one enters into the life that God intends to give us in Jesus. There appear to be two ways that John conceives of this. One is that the person makes a volitional choice to believe in Jesus (which we have already discussed as involving a lifelong relationship of trusting, knowing, obeying, and abiding). The other way John portrays this issue is that it is the work of the Spirit that ushers a person into the new life that God intends. This tension is especially apparent in Jesus's conversation with Nicodemus in John 3. English translations make it more difficult to pick up on, but when Jesus tells Nicodemus in verse 3 that "unless one is born ἄνωθεν (*anothen*) he cannot see the kingdom of God," John uses a verb that carries two meanings. *Anothen* can either mean *again, a second time* or it can mean *from above*.[61] Some scholars suggest that John intentionally used multiple layers of meaning throughout his Gospel, and in this particular passage, Gail O'Day even suggests that Jesus intended for his saying to be misunderstood by Nicodemus, so that he could help move Nicodemus into a new understanding.[62] As he leads Nicodemus into understanding that entering the kingdom necessitates being born from above and being born again, Jesus uses another word with multiple meanings (*pneuma*), which can be translated as *breath, wind,* or *spirit*. The work of God that is

59. Smith, *Theology of the Gospel of John*, 149.

60. Witherington, *John's Wisdom*, 212.

61. O'Day, *Word Disclosed*, 19.

62. Ibid.

involved in this birthing experience is emphasized by Jesus's comparison of the spirit to the wind, which cannot actually be seen, but the effects of which are often easily observable. The emphasis, therefore, according to O'Day, is on helping Nicodemus break out of his customary paradigms and open himself to the new possibilities that God wants to create and give him through Jesus. The emphasis on the exaltation (another word with multiple meanings: *hupsoo*) of Jesus on the cross in verse 14 assists Nicodemus in understanding the strong dimension of divine participation in this process, so that "the point of origin for the one now born is with Jesus, not with ourselves."[63] O'Day addresses the tension between human effort and divine initiative by suggesting that there is a human work of faith involved, but that the intent of this work of faith "is to allow ourselves to be fed by Jesus." This is not easy work for us, however, because we want to hold on to our sense of self-sufficiency and our desire for accomplishment, and this blocks our ability and openness to receive what God wants to give.[64]

Craig Koester also notes John's use of *anothen* and *pneuma* in the Nicodemus story, and he agrees with O'Day that the stronger emphasis is on God's action in the life-giving process. He cautions us, however, not to take Jesus's words in verse 6 ("that which is born of the flesh is flesh, and that which is born of the Spirit is spirit") to suggest that flesh is inherently evil. Jesus's incarnation makes it plain that this is not the case, for if flesh were inherently evil, Jesus would not have come in fleshly form. Though flesh is not inherently evil, Koester suggests, it is nonetheless limited. This means that "flesh can generate relationships in its own sphere, but not human relationships with God, which are of another order. Such relationships occur only when God initiates contact with people in a life-giving way."[65] This does not, however, invalidate the role of human response to God's initiative,

63. O'Day, *Word Disclosed*, 28–29.

64. Ibid., 122. In the U.S. American context, there is strong emphasis on doing rather than being. Steward and Bennett (*American Cultural Patterns*, 69) suggest that "doing is the dominant form of activity for Americans." Moreover, U.S. Americans place a high value on achievement, to the point that "the achievement motivation predominates in America" (Althen and Bennett, *American Ways*, 21). These insights strongly confirm the point that O'Day is making here. It is very difficult for U.S. Americans to conceive of receiving a benefit as valuable as being born again and from above without thinking that we have done something ourselves to achieve that benefit.

65. Koester, *Word of Life*, 137–8.

for Koester goes on to say that it is only through faith that we "partake of the crucified Jesus."[66]

The presence of both human and divine involvement in the life-giving and life-receiving process is not limited in John's Gospel to the Nicodemus story. One may consider, for example, the changing of water to wine in John 2. After Mary insisted that Jesus do something to correct the shortage of wine, he changed water into wine. This divine involvement is emphasized even more strongly by John's comment that Jesus manifested his glory through this sign (verse 11). At the same time, however, John follows his comment about Jesus manifesting his glory with the statement that his disciples believed in him. We thus clearly observe both divine and human involvement in this instance of persons believing.

The same is true of the healing of the official's son in the latter part of chapter 4. The official initiated the encounter by going to Jesus and asking him to heal his son. Jesus then healed his son from a distance, which illustrates divine involvement, and the eventual response to this divine involvement was that the man "himself believed, and all his household."[67]

In chapter 6, we encounter the feeding of the five thousand from five loaves and two fish, which obviously illustrates divine involvement. In the ensuing discourse, Jesus speaks clearly to the reality of human involvement in the life-giving and life-receiving process when he says that the "work" people must do is to believe in him (verse 29).

I propose that this brief excursion into the relationship between divine initiative and human response in John's Gospel is an important one because it has such strong implications for evangelistic theory and practice. If we lean too heavily in the direction of human response, we may be tempted to see evangelism as a primarily human work that is, therefore, mostly devoid of the Spirit's presence, power, and initiative. Conversely, if we lean too heavily in the direction of divine initiative, we may be tempted to see evangelism as a primarily divine work that does not or should not include human participation. Neither of these perspectives is faithful to the biblical portrayal of evangelism, nor more specifically to John's portrayal. There is a strong tendency among evangelistically minded Christians to lean too heavily in the direction of divine initiative at the expense of human involvement in evangelism, so I will limit my comments to that issue.

66. Koester, *Word of Life*, 208.
67. John 4:53.

We may address this issue from at least two perspectives: that of the non-believer who is moving toward a decision to believe, know, obey, and abide in Jesus; and that of other persons whom God may choose to use in the process that leads that person toward this decision. From the perspective of the non-believer's journey toward belief, one of the gravest errors that Christians make is to de-emphasize the need for persons to *respond* to God's initiative. There is such a strong emphasis on God's work in the evangelizing process that we forget that the person must respond to God's work in his or her life, and we therefore fail to *invite* persons to respond to the good news of Jesus's offer of life. This lack of invitation is in direct contrast to the biblical portrayal. In the Synoptic Gospels, for example, Jesus not only proclaimed that the kingdom of God was at hand, but he also preceded that proclamation with the call to repent (Matt 3:2 and Mark 1:15). In Deuteronomy, Moses went to great lengths to explain to the Hebrew people the options of life and death as they relate to following God's ways, but he did not stop with a declaration. He also included an invitation and encouragement to respond: "therefore choose life."[68] In 2 Corinthians, Paul says that "we are ambassadors for Christ, God making his appeal through us. We implore you on behalf of Christ, be reconciled to God."[69]

Returning to John's Gospel, this is seen clearly in his closing purpose statement: "Now Jesus did many other signs in the presence of the disciples, which are not written in this book; but these are written so that you may believe that Jesus is the Christ, the Son of God, and that by believing you may have life in his name."[70] The *so that* phrase clearly indicates that John desires that his readers not simply digest historical information about Jesus, but that they respond to Jesus's call to believe, know, obey, and abide in him. John's understanding of *so that* is seen in the very beginning of his Gospel too, in his comment about John the Baptist: "There was a man sent from God, whose name was John. He came as a witness, to bear witness about the light, that all might believe through him."[71] To offer one more example from John, we note that in the Lazarus story in chapter 11, prior to going to Bethany, Jesus says to the disciples, "Lazarus has died, and for your sake I am glad that I was not there, so that you may believe. But let us go to

68. Deut 30:19.
69. 2 Cor 5:20.
70. John 20:31.
71. John 1:6–7.

him."[72] It is clear in John's Gospel that Jesus's listeners and John's readers are invited to a response of believing. Invitation and response are intrinsic to evangelism. They should not be considered optional. As Lathem writes, "the Gospel (Good News) is an invitation, a call to action, a converting word. All of these demand a response. Indifference, neutrality and silence are not options."[73]

Let us now consider human involvement in evangelism process from the perspective of persons whom God may use in the process of leading non-believers toward believing. First, there is no question that evangelism begins with God. Evangelism has its root in the loving and relational character of God as expressed in the Trinity. God as Father is compassionate toward God's creation and yearns for all of creation, including human beings, to be restored to the life-giving relationship with God that was originally intended in God's creative work. God as Son has come to earth to make it possible for that restoration to take place. God as Spirit leads the evangelizing process, working in the lives of non-Christians to help them become aware of the possibility of new life in Jesus and empowering them to turn toward him, accept his grace, and totally reorient their lives toward him and his ways, and, thus, receive life. God wants us all to be reconciled with God through Christ and experience the new life that he came to give. God yearns for the restoration of God's originally intended relationship with us. In this sense, God is both the prime and primary evangelist.

Evangelism begins with God, but God also intends, invites, and desires that God's people be active participants in the evangelization process. The Scriptures vividly portray that God's plan for calling God's fallen creation back to God's self includes people as integral ministry partners in this work. From the calling of Abraham to be a blessing to all the families of the earth, to young Mary giving birth to the Son, to the early disciples leading thousands of people to Christ—the Bible makes it clear that God wants to communicate the possibility of new life in Jesus to people through people. Therefore, though evangelism begins with God and is utterly dependent on God, God also envisions a vital role for Christians. Without question, God is the sole source of new life in Christ. However, this does not automatically mean that God is the sole agent in the process that leads us to this new life. God's sovereignty in evangelism does not cancel out God's intention for us

72. John 11:14–15.
73. Lathem and Dunn, *Preaching for a Response*, 6.

to be used as God's agents in evangelism. Rather, it is in God's sovereignty that God has chosen us as God's agents.

Charles Finney addresses this issue. He notes that telling Christians they do not need to evangelize since God is the one who brings about new life would be similar to telling a farmer that he or she did not need to plow or sow or weed or harvest, because God would decide whether to cause the crops to grow; the farmer's participation (agency) in God's work would be an infringement on God's sovereignty. Should farmers begin to practice farming in this manner, Finney suggests, the whole world would be reduced to starvation. Finney does not discount God's sovereignty in the process of conversion. He acknowledges that no one can be converted without God's blessing. However, in the process of conversion, he maintains that there are always at least two agents (God and the sinner), and sometimes three (another person besides the sinner—the evangelist), and there is also always one instrument (the truth). Thus, while God's role is the most important one in the conversion process, it is not the only one.[74]

Some persons might suggest that this acknowledgement of the human role in evangelism is mostly limited to persons from the Arminian/Wesleyan theological family. Writing from a Calvinistic perspective, however, J. I. Packer notes that the truth of God's sovereignty in evangelism and the truth of the human role must be accepted on faith, even if they appear to our rational minds to be contradictory. Each principle is solidly scriptural, and so we should simply accept them as God's truth even though we may not understand how they fit together. Regarding evangelism more specifically, Packer suggests that even people who believe strongly in God's sovereignty in election must hold to the scriptural view that we are responsible for our participation in evangelism. "The command to evangelize is a part of God's law. It belongs to God's revealed will for His people. It could not, then, in principle be affected in the slightest degree by anything that we might believe about God's sovereignty in election and calling."[75] Not only should our view of God's sovereignty not inhibit our commitment to evangelism, but Packer goes on to propose that God's sovereignty is the primary motivation *for* our evangelism. It is because we know that God in God's sovereignty has made it possible for persons to be saved that we can be certain our evangelism will bear fruit. "So far from making evangelism pointless, the

---

74. Finney, *Lectures on Revival of Religion*, 13–15.

75. Packer, *Evangelism and the Sovereignty of God*, 96.

sovereignty of God in grace is the one thing that prevents evangelism from being pointless."[76]

Finney and Packer help us immensely regarding the relationship between God's sovereignty and evangelism. Misunderstanding this relationship is not the sole cause of evangelistic apathy among Christians, but it is certainly one of them. We are not responsible for another person's decision to accept God's offer of new life in Christ, but we are responsible for our role as agents that God may want to use to bring persons to a point in their lives where that decision is for them a viable one. We recall those haunting words from Ezekiel 33:7–8: "So you, son of man, I have made a watchman for the house of Israel. Whenever you hear a word from my mouth, you shall give them warning from me. If I say to the wicked, O wicked one, you shall surely die, and you do not speak to warn the wicked to turn from his way, that wicked person shall die in his iniquity, but his blood I will require at your hand.[77] Just as John wrote his gospel so that other persons might believe in Jesus, and through believing, experience new life in him, so too should all Christians be encouraged to develop a strong desire to participate in the evangelizing process, through the guidance and the power of the Holy Spirit.

Individual or Communal?

There is an additional issue from John's Gospel: the relationship between the individual nature and the communal nature of the Jesus-following life. Some biblical scholars suggest that of all the New Testament authors, John focuses the most on the call of individual persons to believe, know, obey, and abide in Jesus, with very little emphasis on the communal nature of Christ-following. This sentiment is based in large part on the lack of references in John's Gospel to the church, church structure, or church order. Raymond Brown, however, warns us that we should be careful not to make too many assumptions about John's ecclesiology based on what he did *not* say in his Gospel (sometimes referred to as an "argument from silence"). Just because John did not address ecclesiology in the same manner as Paul or Peter does not necessarily mean that John had little regard for the communal nature of Christian believing and Christian living.

---

76. Packer, *Evangelism and the Sovereignty of God*, 106.

77. Ezek 33:7–8.

There is no question that John wishes to emphasize that individual persons are called and invited to believe, know, obey, and abide in Jesus, and in so doing receive new life. At the same time, however, John strongly emphasizes the unity of believers and Jesus's insistence that they love one another. The love theme is made very clear in John 13 when Jesus tells the disciples: "A new commandment I give to you, that you love one another: just as I have loved you, you also are to love one another. By this all people will know that you are my disciples, if you have love for one another."[78] Likewise, Jesus emphasizes the unity focus in his prayer to the Father in chapter 17, where he asks the Father to "keep them in your name, which you have given me, that they may be one, even as we are one."[79] In John's Gospel, therefore, is believing, knowing, obeying, and abiding in Jesus an individual affair or a communal affair? The answer is yes and yes. As Brown phrases it, "there was no sharp distinction between community and personal union with Jesus. The foundation of community is the response of individuals to Jesus as the revealer of God and the unique way to God, but those individuals form a unity."[80]

The importance of maintaining an appropriate relationship between personally relating with Jesus and communally relating with both fellow believers and with non-believers has long been an emphasis of the Wesleyan theological family, and this stems from Wesley himself. In his sermon on Matthew 5:13–16 (salt of the earth, light of the world), he argues that if someone would try to live as a Christ-follower in a manner that completely separated them from other people, they would not merely experience a less-than-full Christian life, but they would in fact not be experiencing Christian living at all. Wesley insisted that "When I say, 'This is essentially a social religion,' I mean not only that it cannot subsist so well, but that it cannot subsist at all, without society,—without living and conversing with other men . . . to turn this religion into a solitary one is to destroy it."[81] John Wesley and the author of John's Gospel are in agreement at this point.

78. John 13:34–35.

79. John 17:11.

80. Brown, *Introduction to the Gospel of John*, 226.

81. Wesley, Sermon 24, 241.

What About the Cross?

Prior to concluding our journey into insights from John's Gospel, we would be wise to consider the Johannine perspective on the cross and the cross's relationship to atonement. An enormous amount of material has been written on these topics through the years, and we do not have time or space to deal with even a small portion of that content. To help us navigate the aspects of John's perspective on the cross and atonement that are most pertinent to this project's focus on life, I will frame this discussion around a "conversation" that takes place between Craig Koester and Gail R. O'Day in a 2005 publication of Johannine studies. Koester suggests that we should think about John's treatment of the crucifixion using four frames of reference: "as an expression of love in human terms, as a sacrifice for sin, as conflict with evil, and as a revelation of divine glory."[82]

In his discussion of the crucifixion as a sacrifice for sin, Koester argues that in John's Gospel sin has primarily to do with alienation, unbelief, and the actions that result from unbelief. Referring to John 1:29 ("Behold, the Lamb of God, who takes away the sin of the world!"), he says that this taking away of sin refers to the removal of unbelief. "If sin is a deadly alienation from God, then faith is a lifegiving relationship with God, and the death of Christ takes sin away when it moves people from sin into faith."[83] In this sense, then, *atonement* in John refers not to a sacrifice that satisfies divine justice, but rather to a defeat of unbelief by engendering belief. Koester agrees with other scholars that the death of Jesus is a sacrificial death, but he advocates that this does not automatically necessitate that we think of that sacrificial death as vicarious or substitutionary. Vicarious and/ or substitutionary death revolves around the principal ideas of justice and mercy or law and grace, so that the "price" that should be paid by the sinner is instead paid by Jesus through his death on the cross. Koester believes that this understanding of Jesus's death is not what John has in mind. Rather, "when the love of God, revealed through the death of Jesus, overcomes the sin of unbelief by evoking faith it delivers people from the judgment of God by bringing them into true relationship with God. This is atonement in the Johannine sense."[84] The emphasis is more on the human need for belief than the human need for divine justice.

82. Koester, "Death of Jesus and the Human Condition," 141–57.
83. Ibid., 146.
84. Ibid., 147.

Victory over evil is another frame of reference, that Koester explores, based in large part on John 12:31–33: "'Now is the judgment of this world; now will the ruler of this world be cast out. And I, when I am lifted up from the earth, will draw all people to myself.' He said this to show by what kind of death he was going to die." Koester believes that these verses interpret Jesus's death on the cross in terms of liberating people from the power of evil, so that in this context the issue is "not so much human sin as it is the oppressive power of evil."[85] Ultimately, therefore, each person is faced with the decision to choose between the ruler of this world and the crucified Jesus. Where will our loyalty lie in the cosmic battle between God and evil? This becomes the crucial question. In the sacrifice for sin frame of reference, the person is invited to move from unbelief to belief, and in the victory over evil frame of reference they are invited to claim God as their only ruler. In the sacrifice for sin frame of reference, belief is the human need that the crucifixion addresses; in the victory over evil frame of reference, liberation is the human need that the crucifixion addresses.

In Jesus's prayer in John 17 (among other passages), Koester sees another important frame of reference: the revelation of divine glory. The human need that is addressed here is the need to know God. This is based on Koester's contention that though in John's Gospel *glory* sometimes refers to honor (e.g., in 5:41), it also refers to the nature of revelation. "God's presence is hidden until God chooses to reveal it. The theme of glory has to do with the way revelation takes place."[86] He connects this belief with the signs in John's Gospel. The signs are a revelation of God's glory because they demonstrate God's power. The crucifixion is a revelation of God's glory because it demonstrates God's love. "If glory defines what the crucifixion is, the crucifixion defines what glory is."[87]

The link between the crucifixion and God's love is amplified even more fully in Koester's first frame of reference: love in human terms. He believes that John's Gospel emphasizes the self-giving nature of God's love in the crucifixion: "Greater love has no one than this, that someone lay down his life for his friends."[88] This is something that all of John's readers could immediately understand, and the self-giving, serving nature of this love is strongly reinforced by Jesus's washing of the disciples' feet in John 13. Koester pro-

85. Koester, "Death of Jesus and the Human Condition," 149.
86. Ibid., 151.
87. Ibid., 153.
88. John 15:13.

poses that John's depiction of the crucifixion within this frame of reference demonstrates that for love to be given to others it must be given in ways they can grasp. Additionally, it shows God's desire for love to be lived in human terms. "Since Jesus' love is the source and norm for Christian discipleship, he gives his love in tangible worldly forms so that his disciples might give their love in tangible worldly forms."[89]

Koester's different frames of reference are quite useful, for they help us grasp the different emphases we find in John's Gospel concerning the crucifixion. His frames of reference also coordinate nicely with the way we have observed that John conceives of Christian life in terms of believing, knowing, obeying, and abiding. The sacrifice for sin frame of reference emphasizes the human need to believe, so this clearly ties the crucifixion to the Johannine emphasis on believing. The victory over evil frame of reference highlights the human need for liberation, which Jesus addresses in his healing of sick persons, restoring sight to blind persons, raising dead persons, and feeding hungry persons. In this sense, therefore, the crucifixion validates the liberation from the powers of evil that is intended to be a part of the experience of Christian living. The revelation of divine glory frame of reference speaks directly to the human need to know God, and we have seen many examples of how vital knowing God is to John's understanding of Christian life, to the point that he describes it as eternal life (17:3). The love in human terms frame of reference ties it all together, for we see in the cross that all the rich meanings of the crucifixion rest on the foundation of God's love for us, and we further see that part of Christian obedience involves loving others.

With these connections in mind, it is evident that while some of John's perspectives on the crucifixion and atonement may be different from those of Paul, they are yet quite consistent with the rest of John's Gospel, and they offer strong corroboration for the Johannine emphasis on life. John also shares with Paul a core belief that God's love is evidenced through the crucifixion in a way that demonstrates both our need for a real change that only God can provide, as well as the possibility of that real change taking place if we will only acknowledge our need for it and accept the life that Jesus came to bring.[90]

89. Koester, "Death of Jesus and the Human Condition," 145.

90. T. W. Manson (*On Paul and John,* 121) writes that "what both Paul and John maintain is that there are two factors which are necessary to meet the situation in which man [*sic*] is: an act of God for man's [*sic*] deliverance and the humble recognition on man's [*sic*] part that he is sinful and helpless and must cast himself on this proffered

Earlier I referenced four clusters of questions that this project would deal with, and one of those clusters has to do with our understanding of gospel. What is the good news? What is good about the good news? In inviting others to Christ, what is it that we are inviting non-Christians toward? What are we asking them to embrace? Koester's multiple frames of reference help us think through these questions from John's perspective. In John's Gospel, we are invited to believe in Jesus, to know and obey him, and to abide in him. In so doing, we experience a strong measure of the life of the age to come, and we anticipate experiencing this life yet even more fully after physical death. The crucifixion confirms how profound Jesus's love for us is, and the exaltation that takes place at the crucifixion confirms how deeply God the Father shares in this love. We see at Calvary that God is indeed quite serious in God's desire that we experience a full and vital life of believing, knowing, obeying, and abiding. We are people loved by God, and we are people who should joyfully share that love with others and invite (and help) them to experience the full life that we experience through Jesus.

Gail R. O'Day approaches the issue of God's love as portrayed in John's Gospel in a very different manner. She affirms that Koester's frames of reference are useful in helping us understand John's perspectives on the crucifixion, but she suggests that the crucifixion is not John's primary concern. Much more than Jesus's death, she contends, John is interested in Jesus's life. The central idea that captures John's interest is not the crucifixion, but the incarnation. "Jesus did not die to make God's love known: Jesus *lived* to make God's love known."[91] The "Word made flesh" is introduced quickly in John's Gospel (in the prologue) and Jesus's claim to be one with the Father remains an emphasis throughout. John's major focus, therefore, is not on how Jesus's death brings us life, but on how Jesus's life brings us life. Equally important, according to O'Day, is the Johannine emphasis in 1:16 on the fullness we receive of grace upon grace. This teaches us that John perceives Jesus's incarnation as one of fullness and grace, as distinct from Paul's understanding, which in Philippians 2 focuses on the sacrificial emptying that took place in the incarnation. O'Day does not suggest that Paul's emphasis is inappropriate, but she laments that his understanding "dominates most Protestant conversations about the life and death of Jesus," and this prevents us from discerning that "for John the incarnation is not an emptying: it is

mercy."

91. O'Day, "Love of God Incarnate," 158–67.

a moment of fullness."[92] Regarding atonement, therefore, O'Day believes that Jesus's life, of which his death is a part, "is the locus of revelation and redemption." She even goes so far as to say that "Jesus' death is not necessary to redeem humanity, he redeems flesh by becoming flesh."[93]

To provide an exegetical foundation for her claims, O'Day offers a brief treatment of John 3:16, in which she asserts that this verse centers on God's love in the incarnation, as opposed to the common understanding that this verse primarily revolves around the giving up of Jesus to death. This assertion is based in part on John's use of *monogenes* (*only* in ESV, *only begotten* in KJV, and *one and only* in NIV) in verses 16 and 18, which are the only two verses in which he uses this word outside the prologue. This is a reference to "the birth and generation metaphor field," and this birth and generation language is consistent with the preceding context of Jesus's conversation with Nicodemus, in which he has already discussed the need to be born again and from above. The birth and generation connection between John 3:16 and the incarnation references in the prologue leads O'Day to suggest, therefore, that this verse far more stresses that eternal life is connected to Jesus's life than to Jesus's death. "One is not required to see a reference to the giving up to death; rather, the Johannine context leads one to see instead the full gift of the incarnation as that which makes eternal life possible."[94]

O'Day goes on to point out how this understanding helps us more accurately discern the ways that John integrates Jesus's life and death into his telling of the gospel story. This integration, for example, leads to John's eucharistic material being presented in the middle of Jesus's ministry in chapter 6, incorporated in the Bread of Life conversations following the feeding of the five thousand. With this context providing the theological background, John reconfigures the eucharistic meal "as the feast of the living bread, not the feast of betrayal and death. Jesus' life, not solely his death, is celebrated and experienced in the eucharistic meal. The host of the eucharistic meal provides a superabundance of gifts that surpasses the needs and expectations of those who are present for the feeding. The radical interpretation of the eucharistic traditions that John makes in chapter 6 presents the eucharistic meal as a sacrament of the incarnation, a meal of Jesus' living presence for the community."[95]

92. Ibid., 159.
93. O'Day, "Love of God Incarnate," 160.
94. Ibid., 160–61.
95. Ibid., 166.

How might we assess O'Day's claims? On the one hand, it is true that John's Gospel gives great prominence to the incarnation and the resulting emphasis on life. This emphasis on life is obviously consistent with the life-based focus of this book and provides a strong underpinning for the life-based theory and practice of evangelism. O'Day affirms that "John envisions the possibility of grace and new life that come from fullness, not emptiness and sacrifice, from an image of God that creates new possibilities out of the stuff of human flesh, from love that dwells incarnate."[96] There is great value in inviting persons to the new possibilities that exist for them through a life of believing, knowing, obeying, and abiding in Jesus, so in this sense O'Day's insistence that we include incarnational thinking in theological conversation (to which I would add evangelistic conversation) is noteworthy.

She travels too far afield, however, regarding the relationship of Jesus's death to redemption. When she writes that "Jesus' death is not necessary to redeem humanity," O'Day loses the very integration that she applauds in John. Yes, John emphasizes the Word made flesh. Yes, John places a strong value on Jesus's life. Yes, we should go beyond Pauline understandings of the incarnation, crucifixion, and atonement. At the same time, however, we cannot appropriately speak of redemption and/or atonement without reference to Jesus's death, and John does not attempt to do so. This is made quite plain in John's early inclusion of the "Lamb of God" references that John the Baptist makes to Jesus (1:29 and 1:36), which many of his readers would associate with the sacrificial language of the Levitical code. It is further reinforced by Jesus's references to the laying down of his life for the sheep (10:11, 15, 17) and to Jesus's chapter 6 reference to his flesh being the bread of life that he gives for the world (6:51). Moreover, we can point to John's chapter 11 inclusion of Caiaphas's statement: "'You know nothing at all. Nor do you understand that it is better for you that one man should die for the people, not that the whole nation should perish.' He did not say this of his own accord, but being high priest that year he prophesied that Jesus would die for the nation, and not for the nation only, but also to gather into one the children of God who are scattered abroad."[97]

The best way forward, therefore, is to combine the insights from Koester's multiple frames of reference with O'Day's emphasis on Jesus's life and incarnation. In this context, we may view the crucifixion and atonement in

96. O'Day, "Love of God Incarnate," 167.
97. John 11:49–52.

terms of how they fit into the comprehensive Johannine picture of who Jesus is. John's Gospel presents a portrayal of the pre-incarnational Jesus who was God (and was with God); the incarnational Jesus who came to earth in fullness to help us know him; the wise and powerful Jesus who taught, healed, raised, and fed; the compassionate Jesus who died to demonstrate the depth of God's love; and the resurrected and exalted Jesus who gives us the Holy Spirit to guide us in how to continue abiding in him (Jesus), and in so doing experience full and vital life. The crucifixion and atonement, therefore, are indeed important to John, but they are important within the larger framework of John's portrayal of Jesus and should not be separated from that comprehensive framework. Likewise, the crucifixion and atonement should not be removed from that framework. We are invited to full life in Jesus, and that full life is directly linked to the fullness of who Jesus is and was, as well as what he experienced in our stead and on our behalf. This implies that the ministry of evangelism must be envisioned in a comprehensive fashion. I will explore this theme more fully in chapter 8.

5

Theological Insights Regarding the Life Theme

IN THE PREVIOUS TWO chapters, we focused on insights from the field of
biblical studies, with primary emphasis on selected Old Testament scholars and a journey into the Gospel of John. In this chapter, I will broaden
the field of inquiry to include theologians and anthropologists who can
provide us additional understandings concerning the evangelistic implications of a strong focus on the biblical theme of life. An important
consideration at the outset is that the fields of theology and anthropology
overlap at various points; this makes sense given the holistic nature of God
and God's creation (including human persons). As one delves into these
materials, it also becomes quickly obvious that anthropology seriously
impacts evangelistic theory and practice; or, perhaps it would be better to
say that it *should* do so. Our understanding of what it means to be human
relates to our understanding of what it is that God has in mind for us in
offering us new life in Jesus. Ray Anderson phrases it this way: "The essential nature of human beings is determinative for our understanding of
the kind of redemption God has wrought for human beings through his
Son, Jesus Christ."[1] Whether evangelism scholars and practitioners have
paid sufficient attention to anthropological insights in the past is subject
to debate, but in this chapter those insights will be linked with the theory
and practice of evangelism.

The chapter begins with three theologians who accentuate life in their
theology: Karl Barth, Jurgen Moltmann, and Thomas Oden. This is followed by a brief survey of material from three additional theologians who
include an explicit anthropological perspective in their work: David Kelsey,
Ray Anderson, and Paul Hiebert. The goal is to discover pertinent issues

---

1. Anderson, *On Being Human*, 70.

related to the biblical theme of life and its implications for the theory and practice of evangelism. I then introduce insights from other theologians related to those issues.

Theological Insights from Barth, Moltmann, and Oden

Karl Barth

In the "Doctrine of Creation" section of the second volume of *Church Dogmatics*, Karl Barth offers valuable theological insights concerning the theme of life. Three in particular stand out. The first is the way Barth grounds our understanding of life in our relationship with and commitment to God. This helps us avoid the trap of so fully embracing life that we begin to embrace it as an entity in and of itself, separate from God who created us. Barth reminds us that "life is no second God, and therefore the respect due to it cannot rival the reverence owed to God."[2] Yes, we respect life. Yes, we must do all we can to preserve life and help others experience life as God intends. But that is precisely the point: it is life as God intends, not life as we or others intend.

Anthropologically speaking, Barth observes that human beings are not constituted in any way distinct from God, but rather are constituted directly in relationship to God who has created them and given them freedom to live. "Life as such thus means to live for the One to whom it belongs and from whom it has been received as a loan."[3] This may seem to be a simple theological point, but it is a crucial one nonetheless, for it reminds us that as we investigate the evangelistic implications of a strong emphasis on the biblical theme of life, we are not trying to portray and invite people to a fullness of life that is experienced apart from God, but rather we are inviting them to a fullness of life that can only be experienced in an intimate, reverential, and obedient relationship with God. This helps our life focus remain Jesus-focused.

A second emphasis for Barth is one that has already emerged in this project: life is experienced in relationships, most particularly in our vertical relationship with God and our horizontal relationships with others. Again speaking anthropologically, Barth cautions us that we must never conceive of human persons as being somehow "determined" apart from

2. Barth, *Church Dogmatics*, 2/4: *The Doctrine of Creation*, 342.
3. Ibid., 330.

those relationships. It is not that John Doe as a human being has relationships with God and other people that are distinct from his "being-ness." Rather, John Doe's relationships with God and other people are in part determinative of his "being-ness." A human person "is first for God and his fellow-man [*sic*], and then and for this reason he exists as this being in accordance with his determination."[4]

In addition to our relating with God and other people, Barth also believes it is necessary to grasp the role of the created order as the "indispensable living background" in which we live. This reminds us that though the world of plants and animals is provided for our use, we are neither the owners nor the creators of it. God and God alone is the creator and owner of the created order.[5] This living background, therefore, adds another dimension to our relational understanding of life, which means that evangelistic portrayals and/or invitations should consider ways to include references to our relationships with God, other people, and the created world.

A third emphasis Barth offers is that "the will for life is also the will for joy, delight and happiness."[6] He mentions the large number of biblical references to "delight, joy, bliss, exultations, merry-making, and rejoicing," and then further suggests that this joy is "genuine, earthly, human joy: the joy of harvest, wedding, festival and victory; the joy not only of the inner but also the outer man [*sic*]; the joy in which one may and must drink wine as well as eat bread, sing and play as well as speak, dance as well as pray."[7] This embracing of joy, delight, and happiness is not to be envisioned as a hedonistic pleasure-seeking apart from God, but rather something that flows out of a deep sense of gratitude for the gift of life that God has granted us. In this sense, then, our joy, delight, and happiness are a form of praise and thanksgiving to God. Barth also highlights that joy is a relational affair, so that we should continually ask ourselves what will give joy to other persons and try to help them experience that joy.[8] Our joy, therefore, is more fully realized when we help others experience their own joy, and our joy should never come at the expense of other persons.

An additional important point is that Barth does not conceive of this as a happy-go-lucky joy that ignores suffering and hardship. He observes

4. Barth, *Church Dogmatics*, 2/4, 324–25.
5. Ibid., 350–1.
6. Ibid., 375.
7. Ibid., 376.
8. Ibid., 379.

that "a true and good joy is that we do not evade the shadow of the cross of Jesus Christ and are not unwilling to be genuinely joyful even as we bear the sorrows laid upon us."[9]

A final point for Barth is that our joy, delight, and happiness are provisional. We are happy and joyful in this life out of a deep sense of gratitude for the opportunity to live and be in relationship with God and others. Additionally, we are happy and joyful in this life because we know that an even greater joy and delight await us in eternity. There is a symbiotic relationship, therefore, between our anticipation of what is yet to come and our experience of full, joyful living in the here and now.[10]

Jurgen Moltmann

Jurgen Moltmann also places a strong emphasis on life in his theology. In *The Passion for Life: A Messianic Lifestyle*, he states that people are apathetic toward life, and that love is the "antidote" for this apathy. Because love is most fully expressed in Jesus's sacrifice at Calvary, it is through following his example of loving self-sacrifice that we most fully experience the vigorous and abundant life that God intends for us. This in turn leads to a stress on the role of human relationships in our following of the messianic lifestyle. Sacrificial love does not take place in a relational vacuum, but by its very definition requires participation in human community. "Hope is lived, and it comes alive, when we go outside of ourselves and, in joy and pain, take part in the lives of others. It becomes concrete in open community with others."[11]

In addition to this recurring theme of relationships, Moltmann highlights another recurring theme, an emphasis on life before death as opposed to life after death. "Jesus' life is inspired not just by the wish for a life *after* death, but by the will for life *before* death, yes even *against* death. Where the sick are healed, lepers are accepted, and sins are not punished but forgiven, there *life* is present. Freed life, redeemed life, divine life is there, in this world, in our times, in the midst of us."[12]

Moltmann also highlights the life-now emphasis in a book he wrote twenty years later, in which he asserts an intimate relationship between the

9. Barth, *Church Dogmatics*, 2/4, 383.
10. Ibid., 384–5.
11. Moltmann, *Passion for Life*, 35.
12. Ibid., 24.

role of the Spirit and the biblical theme of life. In this context, he writes that "people who ask for the Holy Spirit to come to us—in our hearts, into the community we live in, and to our earth—don't want to flee into heaven or to be snatched away into the next world. They have hope for their hearts, their community, and this earth."[13] This does not mean that Spirit-led or Spirit-filled Christians completely ignore the biblically anticipated future. Moltmann affirms that "the future towards which faith is meant to grow and develop reaches forward beyond this human life into God's future, 'the day of Jesus Christ', God's eternal kingdom."[14] But this futuristic orientation does not distract us from stressing the present-day impact that God intends in Christ through the Spirit.

An important added focus by Moltmann in this book is that of God's creation. The Spirit's intention is not only to bring life to (and within) human relationships, but also to do so in a way that honors the bodyliness of human beings as well as the prominence of God's physical earth. "Like the Spirit of creation, the Spirit of the new creation creates communities for living shared by human beings and other living things, just as it creates communities among people. The new creation doesn't abolish bodyliness. It renews it for eternal livingness."[15]

One other theme by Moltmann in this book bears mentioning: he proposes a direct connection between God's mission, the Spirit, and life. "God's mission is nothing less than the sending of the Holy Spirit from the Father through the Son into this world, so that this world should not perish but live. The gospel of John tells us quite simply what it is that is brought in to the world from God through Christ: *life*."[16]

A final book by Moltmann that merits study is *The Church in the Power of the Spirit: A Contribution to Messianic Ecclesiology*. In this book, Moltmann grounds ecclesiology in his interpretation of the synoptic emphasis on Jesus's messianic mission. He construes a direct connection to this messianic mission with the community of the exodus (a new exodus in Christ), with the resulting claim that "healing the sick, liberating the captives, and the hunger for righteousness belong to the mission and go together with the preaching of the gospel to the poor."[17] In this context, *poor* refers to poverty

13. Moltmann, *Source of Life*, 11–12.

14. Ibid., 34.

15. Ibid., 24.

16. Ibid., 19.

17. Moltmann, *Church in the Power of the Spirit*, 76.

that is experienced in some way by all human beings, because it can refer to economic, social, physical, psychological, moral, or religious poverty. We all, therefore, experience the "fellowship of poverty," for we all experience some measure of enslavement and/or dehumanization.[18] Because in Jesus God has come near, all persons are called to "make a fresh start and to free themselves, and this they can do. The gospel itself is the mediation between the coming kingdom of God and the person who is turning to freedom."[19] Moltmann characterizes this fresh start as a turning away from oppression, death, and evil, toward life, righteousness, and freedom.

Important to Moltmann is that this turning must be understood in a holistic way. It is not individual or communal, nor is it religious or political. It impacts all of life in all its spheres. Yes, individuals turn, but they do so within the framework of human relationships. And yes, these newly turned individuals form what we might call a religious body, the church (the community of the new exodus), but the life, righteousness, and freedom that we are turning toward are also to be offered to and experienced by persons outside that community. Just as Jesus's messianic mission had to do with healing, liberation, righteousness, and preaching to the poor (and remember we are all poor in some sense), so too must the mission of individual Christians and the mission of the community of the new exodus include and impact all those dimensions of what God is doing (or at least intends to do) through the New Messiah. The church's goal "is not to spread the Christian religion or to implant the church; it is to liberate the people of the exodus in the name of the coming kingdom."[20]

Moltmann goes on to describe the three "world processes" that this liberation must impact. First is the economic process, with emphasis placed on the need for human beings and nature to be liberated from exploitation. Second is the political process, which has to do primarily with who controls the power. In this regard what is required is freedom from human repression of other human beings. Third is the cultural process, which Moltmann views primarily in terms of educational, racial, and sexual "privileges." The goal here is to end the practice of alienation from other persons based on their education, race, and/or gender.[21]

---

18. Moltmann, *Church in the Power of the Spirit*, 79.

19. Ibid., 80.

20. Ibid., 81–84.

21. Ibid., 164–67.

There is much to value in Moltmann's work. His emphasis on life as central to God's mission and the ministry of the Holy Spirit is helpful, as is his repeated insistence that the life that God brings is not to be limited to any particular area of interest. To the contrary, the life that God intends and brings is to impact every area of life, including personal, relational, political, cultural, religious, and economic spheres. Moreover, this impact is to be felt now, in this life, before death. It is not something that we simply hope for at a future time, but it is something we trust God for now and partner with God's Spirit to help bring about. Accepting and participating in God's offer of life should make a difference now, and it should make a difference in everything: how we relate interpersonally, how we vote, how and where we spend our money, which causes we fight for, which oppressions we oppose, which injustices we battle against, and much more.

Thomas Oden

Thomas Oden is another well-respected and prolific theologian. Included among his works is a three-volume series on systematic theology. Germane to this project is the fact that Oden frames this series around the theme of life. The three volumes are titled *The Living God, The Word of Life*, and *Life in the Spirit*. Of particular interest is Oden's treatment of life as the unifying theme of all Christian theology. He addresses this in his second volume, *The Word of Life*: "Christian theology in summary concerns God's own life, God's life offered for humanity, and our life in God."[22] He notes how 1 John uses "the Word of life" as its principal theme and how that theme parallels the prologue in John's Gospel. He goes on to suggest that this theme (the Word of life) is alluded to by Paul in Philippians 2:16 ("holding fast to the word of life") and is further reinforced with Paul's references to Jesus's life at work in us (2 Cor 4:12), our lives being "hidden with Christ in God" (Col 3:3), and the fact that Jesus is our life (Col 3:4). Additionally, Oden notes that "to Jesus the predicate 'life' has been unreservedly, almost recklessly, ascribed in Scripture." Moreover, Oden suggests that we can see examples in the book of Acts of how prevalent the life theme was in the early preaching of the church (Acts 3:15, Jesus is author of life; Acts 17:25, Jesus gives all people life; and Acts 5:20, the full message of this new life).[23]

22. Oden, *Word of Life*, 431.
23. Ibid., 432–7.

Oden concludes this volume with a treatment of Jesus's resurrection as it relates to apocalyptic hope and combines that treatment with the life theme: "The Christian presently lives a life hid in Christ—born from above by the power of the Spirit, embodying and declaring the good news, going about doing good, willing to die for the truth, living in newness of life and in hope of the resurrection at the last day."[24] We see an obvious emphasis here on the life theme being strongly linked with Jesus.

Oden laid the groundwork for this strong emphasis on the life theme in his first volume, where—like Baab, Eichrodt, and others—Oden emphasizes God as the living God, referring to "God's unutterable aliveness."[25] As the living God, he is "present amid the people in radical, unceasing spontaneity and limitless energy" and is therefore "the source of our life—active and tireless."[26] In his final volume, Oden deals with the role of the Spirit in Christian living, and he reiterates that "the central theme of this systematic theology is life: the living God, the Word of life, life in the Spirit."[27]

Obviously, there is much more to be gleaned from a three-volume series, but these general insights serve well in strengthening the theological foundation for a life-based focus to undergird evangelistic theory and practice. More specifically, I submit that Oden's use of life as the overriding theme of his systematic theology is a good illustration of how vital it is to understand the distinction between goal and instrument or means.

Oden deals with a myriad of theological issues. Examples include omniscience, omnipotence, foreknowledge, holiness, judgment, justice, righteousness, faithfulness, justification, sanctification, atonement, incarnation, and many more. Each of these issues is important to a comprehensive understanding of who God is, who we are, and how we are to live in relation to the gift of life that Christ came to bring. But the ultimate goal, the overarching interest, is life. We are grateful for our justification, but our gratitude is centered in how our justification contributes to our experience of life. We commit ourselves to lives of holiness, but we do this not simply to say that we are holy, but because holiness leads us more fully into an experience of the full life that God intends for us. Life is the goal, and as the goal, it should be reflected in evangelistic theory and practice.

---

24. Oden, *Living God*, 1482.
25. Ibid., 64.
26. Ibid., 65.
27. Ibid., 254.

Offer Them Life

Insights from Kelsey, Anderson, and Hiebert

David Kelsey

In his theological anthropology, David Kelsey observes that three categories of questions are normally addressed in anthropology:

- What are we?

- How ought we to be?

- Who am I and who are we?[28]

There are two contexts that serve as background to anthropological
inquiry: proximate and ultimate. The proximate context has to do with "the
physical and social worlds in which we live." The ultimate context has to do
with the larger, more fundamental context, which for Christians implies
God and how God relates with us.[29] Concerning how God relates with us,
Kelsey proposes that according to the "narrative logic" of the Bible, God
relates to us in three ways: God creates us, God draws us to eschatological consummation, and God reconciles us.[30] Using these three ways as a
comprehensive framework, he develops a theological and anthropological
depiction of how we are to be and live. Within this depiction of how we are
to be and live in response to God's relating with us, five themes in particular
are pertinent to my project:

- Life envisioned as human flourishing

- Human flourishing as it relates to the provisional nature of living on
borrowed breath

- The social, public, and relational nature of our life as part of the
quotidian[31]

- Love to neighbor

- Reconciliation of our estranged proximate contexts through Jesus

28. Kelsey, *Eccentric Existence*, 1–2.

29. Ibid., 4–5.

30. Ibid., 5.

31. Kelsey (*Eccentric Existence*, 190) uses this term to describe what is most often referred to by other people as God's creation, God's created world, and so on. He describes
it as "the lived world . . . the everyday finite realities of all sorts—animal, vegetable, and
mineral—in the routine networks that are constituted by their ordinary interactions."

78

Life Envisioned as Human Flourishing

Kelsey recommends that we base our concept of human flourishing on who the trinitarian God is. He highlights three features of "the community-in-communion that is God's life." First is that Father, Son, and Spirit engage in "reciprocal self-giving" not based on a need for relationship, but based rather on a fullness of being. Second, because of the richness and inexhaustibility of God's life, we cannot grasp it cognitively. Third, Father, Son, and Spirit each choose to relate one with the other. They are not forced to do so, which means that God makes an independent choice to love. Kelsey suggests that human flourishing, therefore, should be thought of in like terms. Human flourishing involves fullness of life, is finally beyond our cognitive ability to grasp, and includes self-determinative choices to relate with and love others.[32]

Based on Job 10, Kelsey further explains his theory of human flourishing by contrasting it with the concept of health.[33] He argues that even persons whose bodies are unhealthy can yet flourish in their relationship with God and others, so the related concepts of healthy, unhealthy, functional, and dysfunctional do not serve well as indicators of human flourishing as he conceives it. Flourishing, however, can mean to blossom and to thrive. Kelsey rejects the use of thrive as an indicator of human flourishing because it lends itself too readily to being viewed as a health-related metaphor. Blossom, therefore, is his preferred image. "'To blossom' is to manifest the type of beauty of which a given life is capable by virtue of God relating to it creatively."[34]

Human Flourishing in Relation to the Provisional Nature of Living on Borrowed Breath

One reason that Kelsey does not want to use health-related metaphors to describe human flourishing is because as persons living on borrowed breath we must consider the finitude of the quotidian. This is a crucial

32. Kelsey, *Eccentric Existence*, 77.

33. Kelsey (*Eccentric Existence*, 100) argues that Genesis 1 through 11 is designed to contribute to the *deliverance* narrative of the Pentateuch, and therefore should not be leaned upon for *creation* theology. The best source for creation theology is the Wisdom literature, because it "is not bent by the narrative logic of the accounts of God's acts of deliverance to which it is ordered."

34. Kelsey, *Eccentric Existence*, 315–8.

understanding for Kelsey, because it reminds us that we should not look back to Eden to develop our concept of human flourishing, nor should we look ahead to some future time when things will be different, nor should we think of it as transcendent to our everyday lives. Rather, real human flourishing takes place in the midst of a quotidian that is living on borrowed breath, a quotidian that is in fact dying. This helps us conceive of a human flourishing that is grounded in who God created us to be in relation to the everyday circumstances in which God has placed us.[35]

An important point here is that unlike much traditional theology, the creation theology reflected in the biblical Wisdom literature does not conceive of the finitude of creation as distinct from God's intention in creation. When we speak of human flourishing, therefore, we are not referring to an ideal notion of a "perfectly actualized human being," but rather to an "ordinary, everyday human person."[36]

The Social, Public, and Relational Nature of Our Life as Part of the Quotidian

Given the language of Kelsey's description of the quotidian as involving "the everyday finite realities of all sorts—animal, vegetable, and mineral—in the routine *networks* that are constituted by their ordinary *interactions*," it is no surprise that he places a strong emphasis on the social, public, and relational nature of our lives, and therefore of human flourishing. He speaks about a "public *Missio Dei*," and contends that God's mission impacts everything related to our public and social contexts.[37] In this regard, therefore, we must not overemphasize our private, subjective experiences with God.[38] Kelsey does not suggest that we ignore our personal experiences in relating with God, but he proposes that God's "eschatological blessing engages the social and cultural dimensions of personal bodies' lives quite as much as it

35. Kelsey, *Eccentric Existence*, 315–6.

36. Ibid., 201–4.

37. Ibid., 481–82, emphasis added.

38. Kelsey (*Eccentric Existence*, 384–401) acknowledges that each person has an "unsubstitutable personal identity," but he favors Michael Welker's position that we must view each person as a "concrete individual" rather than an "abstract individual." The concrete individual's unsubstitutable personal identity is both located in and part and parcel of the proximate context in which he or she is placed, so that we cannot truly speak of who a person "is" without also speaking of their social and public networks of relationships.

does the privacy of their subjective interiorities and the networks of their more psychologically intimate interpersonal relationships."[39]

Love to Neighbor

The love to neighbor dimension of human flourishing is based primarily on Kelsey's interpretation of the Beatitudes, and it involves being with our fellow estranged human creatures and also being for them.[40]

In talking of our being with them, Kelsey states that our estrangement from God has produced proximate contexts that include hatred, violence, and deception. In the midst of these proximate contexts, we are encouraged to share kindness and mourning with an attitude of humility. Humility, therefore, is not passive in nature but active. We actively seek to be with others who share these experiences. We mourn with them, and we share kindness with them. We intentionally seek to be with them.[41]

Being for our fellow estranged human creatures means that not only do we cry kindly with them in our shared proximate contexts, but we also try to do something to change what takes place in those contexts. We attempt to serve as agents in bringing about alleviation of suffering and liberation from oppression.[42]

Reconciliation of Our Estranged Proximate Contexts through Jesus

Kelsey suggests that we live in proximate contexts that can be foundationally described by estrangement.[43] Grounded in his continuing commitment to the Wisdom literature, he maintains that this estrangement is created primarily through our living "foolishly in distorted faith" rather than living "wisely in faith."[44] When faith becomes distorted through foolish living, then sin and evil follow.[45] In a similar fashion to O'Day, Kelsey highlights

---

39. Kelsey, *Eccentric Existence*, 481–82.
40. Ibid., 797–807.
41. Ibid., 797–803.
42. Ibid., 803–10.
43. Ibid., 607.
44. Ibid., 402.
45. Kelsey (*Eccentric Existence*, 402) urges a clear distinction between sin and evil. Sin is defined theocentrically, so that it refers to "a distortion of proper human response to God." Evil is defined from the perspective of the creature, so that it refers to the "violation

the incarnation of Jesus as the key factor in this reconciliation.[46] He suggests that it is through Jesus's living among us and sharing our estranged proximate contexts that Jesus exchanged his "true life" for "our living deaths."[47] Jesus experienced death, and in that sense his death plays a factor in this exchange, but not in as strong a sense as is the case in most theological understandings. His death was to be expected because he was born into the same finite proximate contexts that we are born into. Kelsey, therefore, for example, does not speak in the language of atonement, substitution, or vicarious sacrifice. An exchange indeed takes place, but that exchange is principally expressed through the incarnation, not through the cross.[48]

Ray Anderson

Ray Anderson argues for a stronger move among Christian scholars toward a theological anthropology rather than a nontheological one. The dilemma with nontheological anthropologies is that they begin with humanity rather than with God. Theological anthropology of necessity must begin with humanity too, because human existence is the only possible place to start. The difference, however, is that nontheological anthropologies both start with humanity and seek to have the ultimate say, whereas theological anthropologies start with humanity but also recognize that God has the final word. Hence, the Word of God made flesh becomes the starting place for theological anthropology.[49] Starting with the Word of God, therefore, leads us to an appreciation of the *Imago Dei* for theological anthropology.[50]

Anderson highlights two dimensions of the *Imago Dei*: encounter and relation.[51] God's essential "personhood" is expressed as a we and not an I.[52] As persons created in God's image, therefore, we must recognize that it is part of our essential personhood both to relate with other persons and to

---

of creatures' integrities" that results from sin. Sin is something that we cause through our own distorted response to God, whereas evil is what happens to us as the result of the distorted response of another.

46. Kelsey, *Eccentric Existence*, 607–27.

47. Ibid., 642–6.

48. Ibid., 647.

49. Anderson, *On Being Human*, 5–19.

50. Ibid., 69–73.

51. Ibid., 73–77.

52. Ibid., 73.

know that when we relate with them we encounter God's image in them.[53] Having cast this foundational vision for the place of the image of God in theological anthropology, Anderson proceeds to delineate several implications for human living. The two implications most pertinent to this project are "freedom in dependence" and "creatureliness as natural life."

Freedom in Dependence

God has created us to be free, but this freedom "depends on the source of the Word." This dependence on God reminds us that we have been created by God and summoned into a relationship with God. In this sense our freedom is "self-determining," for it determines who we are in relation to who God is and how God has created us to be in relationship with God and others. We should see our freedom, therefore, as an astounding gift. Through God's gracious gift of creation and summons, we are free to fellowship with God and participate in God's life.[54]

Importantly for Anderson, the freedom we are discussing does not refer to "the autonomy of the human self—a kind of neutrality by which the self exists independently of God's determination."[55] Human dignity is often erroneously founded on freedom of choice, but that is not the freedom God intends, because it "denies dependence on the other as the source of one's own personhood."[56] Pope John Paul II affirms this perspective, noting that too often our notion of freedom is one that "exalts the isolated individual in an absolute way" and fails to grasp "the *inherently relational dimension*" of freedom. This is a freedom that "negates and destroys life," because it loses its connection with God's truth.[57]

---

53. Anderson, *On Being Human*, 74.

54. This paragraph is a summary of Anderson's thoughts concerning "freedom in dependence" (*On Being Human*, 78–82).

55. Anderson, *On Being Human*, 80.

56. Ibid., 78–82.

57. John Paul II, *The Gospel of Life*, 30–37.

Creatureliness as Natural Life[58]

As "sixth-day creatures," human beings share solidarity with the rest of creation, and yet we also experience a tension "between the material and immaterial," for God's breathing into us produced "a creaturely soul" that marks us as also different from the rest of creation. Anderson suggests that Christian theology has tended to overemphasize the "creaturely soul" dimension of our existence to the extent that a nonbiblical separation of soul and body has been conceived. This has led to an inappropriate devaluation of our bodies as essential to our personhood and to an equally illegitimate conception of our souls as immortal. Anderson argues that "to stress immortality as an abstract psychical experience of the self apart from the body is incompatible with biblical anthropology."[59] Our bodies, therefore, far from being "lower" than our souls, are part and parcel of who we are, and who we were created to be, and are included in what God intends for us in Jesus. It is imperative, Anderson contends, that rather than think of our "creatureliness" as unimportant to or disconnected from our experience of full life in Christ, we should see it as an integral part of that full life.[60]

Theological Paradigm for Authentic Personhood

After fleshing out his thoughts concerning the significance of being created in God's image, Anderson then develops a theological paradigm for authentic personhood. The four elements of the paradigm include election (affirmation of the self), covenant (relatedness of the self), salvation/atonement (healing of the self), and eschaton (significance of the self).[61]

58. This section is a summary of important points from Anderson's *On Being Human* (132–5).

59. Anderson, *On Being Human*, 132–4. An attempt at helping us conceive of our essential being as *including* our bodies is one of the reasons that Kelsey refers to human persons as "personal bodies." Kelsey refers to "personal bodies," "personal living bodies," and "living bodies" throughout his work (Kelsey, *Eccentric Existence*, see especially 301–3). We may also recall here Moltmann's contention that "the new creation doesn't abolish bodyliness. It renews it for eternal livingness" (Moltmann, *Source of Life*, 124).

60. Ibid., 139.

61. Ibid., 161–78.

ELECTION (AFFIRMATION OF THE SELF)

The existential human need that election fulfills is the need for me to be affirmed, for someone or something to say yes to my condition. In election we learn that "we can become human because we are in fact divinely determined to be human and are human." Importantly, this being human involves not simply to exist but to exist "as one who bears the divine image and likeness."[62] Thus, we both bear God's image and are chosen by God.

COVENANT (RELATEDNESS OF THE SELF)

Being in relationship with God and others is fundamental to our humanity, and the theological concept of covenant helps address this essential need. We are different from God and others, but this difference is best described as "differentiation of the self within the structure of relation." Covenant, therefore, encourages us to embrace the fact that "our fundamental condition is one of belonging."[63]

SALVATION/ATONEMENT (HEALING OF THE SELF)

There is an existential human need for restoration and healing, and reconciliation is what meets that need. Through Jesus's incarnation and atonement the "ontological foundation for all renewal and healing of persons" is brought about, and this prepares the way for persons to experience full health, which "is not the absence of sickness, but a positive orientation of the self toward the objective hope which results from God's initial intention." Therefore, as we seek the healing of salvation, the crucial question to ask ourselves is not who am I? Rather, we should ask: Where do I belong? Where is the place that promises my healing and affirms my health as a person?[64]

---

62. Anderson, *On Being Human*, 162–7.
63. Ibid., 167–71.
64. Ibid., 172–5.

ESCHATON (SIGNIFICANCE OF THE SELF)

The resurrection of Jesus demonstrates that he is the *eschatos*, the "last one"; this knowledge provides a sense of comfort and hope in this present age. Our comfort and hope are based on faith, however, for Jesus is not physically with us now. As we walk by faith and are empowered by the Spirit, we continue to reach out for the presence of Jesus, and "in that reaching out we encounter a reality which becomes present to us." This in turn enables us to "reorient life to the final event which constitutes the present," and that fulfills the human existential need for significance. Our lives are significant now because in Jesus the *eschatos,* they will be significant then.[65]

Anderson moves from his development of a theological paradigm for authentic personhood to a liturgical paradigm for authentic personhood, with a strong emphasis on the role of community. He contends that Jesus's sharing of life with the disciples throughout his ministry clearly demonstrates that "the fundamental liturgical paradigm of personhood is community," for the "personhood of God himself [*sic*], which is communal by nature, is itself the paradigm of all personhood. And what we call community is the liturgical expression of that personhood experienced as co-humanity."[66] The community of Christ, therefore, is both where and through whom the ministry of Christ takes place in the world.

Especially germane to this project is how Anderson links this community-based emphasis to the ministry of evangelism. He submits that evangelism could be grounded on the fact that a person has value, and that based on that value as communicated through the community, the person could then be invited to believe. From this viewpoint, therefore, it is first through the gift of belonging that a person senses his or her value before God, and it is only after that holy ("I am valuable to God") experience that the person would then be in a position to believe. Anderson suggests that when we divorce evangelism from community and thereby ask the person to believe outside the context of community, any later invitation or encouragement to participate in the community will be conceived of as duty rather than gift. However, when we issue the invitation to believe within the context of an already present life-in-community, then the person who chooses to follow Jesus will much more naturally and easily be able to receive the nurture, support, and encouragement that the community offers.[67]

65. Anderson, *On Being Human*, 175–8.

66. Ibid., 182.

67. Ibid., 186–90. Anderson specifically refers to the Lord's Supper, noting that it

Paul Hiebert

Though Paul Hiebert's primary interest is to equip Christian leaders who serve in intercultural settings, some of his material is nonetheless applicable to this project. Two of Hiebert's points provide a framework for our discussion. The first point is that there are three primary dimensions of culture (cognitive, affective, and evaluative), each of which must be involved in our Christ-following journey.[68] The second point is that the ultimate this-life goal of Christian conversion is to move persons toward embracing a biblical worldview (which is delineated along the cognitive, affective, and evaluative dimensions of culture).[69] Hiebert admits that it is difficult for us to lay claim to understanding *the* biblical worldview, since "our attempts to understand what God has revealed in Scripture are partial and biased by our historical and cultural perspectives." Given this understanding, it is yet imperative that with humility we strive to understand "the structure of truth revealed in Scripture."[70] Within this context of humble striving, Hiebert suggests that the following themes (and their corollary counter-themes) emerge from Scripture as vital to worldview transformation[71]:

- Cognitive themes (beliefs: knowledge, logic, wisdom, perceptions of reality)

- Affective themes (feelings: aesthetics, beauty, likes and dislikes, matters of "taste")

- Evaluative themes (values: good/bad, true/false, right/wrong, allegiances)

The central thrust of these themes taken together is that biblical worldview transformation involves a lifelong journey of Christ-centered relational interactions with God and others that are based in an acknowledgement of God as sole creator and king, and us as those whom God loves and calls into community with God and others. Our relational interactions

---

could be seen as "a liturgical form of evangelism" (189), which he also notes is in agreement with John Wesley's contention that the Lord's Supper is a "converting ordinance."

68. Hiebert, *Anthropological Insights for Missionaries*, 30–34, 265.

69. Hiebert, *Transforming Worldviews*, 9–12.

70. Hiebert, *Anthropological Insights for Missionaries*, 265.

71. Hiebert describes the cognitive, affective, and evaluative dimensions of culture in 30–34 of *Anthropological Insights for Missionaries*, and he discusses the biblical worldview themes that emerge from Scripture in relation to the cognitive, affective, and evaluative dimensions in 268–99 of *Transforming Worldviews*.

with God are to be characterized by holy awe in God's presence. Our relational interactions with others are to be characterized by the fruits of the Spirit, resulting in communities and cultures suffused with shalom, love, and peace. The primary agent for bringing about shalom is the community of God's people.

Following his discussion of the biblical worldview themes that emerge from Scripture in relation to the cognitive/affective/evaluative dimensions of culture, Hiebert examines the nature of transformation. Within this examination, of particular relevance is his treatment of the differences between intrinsic sets and relational sets, plus the differences between digital sets and ratio sets.

Intrinsic Sets versus Relational Sets

A consideration of sets has to do with the way a culture defines categories. *Intrinsic sets* refer to the cognitive placement of someone or something into a particular category based on characteristics that are intrinsic to that person or thing. I, for example, could be placed in the following categories based on who or what I am: male, Caucasian, and adult. *Relational sets*, on the other hand, refer to the cognitive placement of someone or something into a particular category based on who or what the person is related to, rather than who they are in and of themselves. In this case I could be placed in the following categories: father of Chris and John, husband of Nancy, friend of Ralph, and the like. All cultures use both types of sets, but one tends to dominate.[72]

In a culture where intrinsic category formation is more prevalent, the category of Christian will tend to be defined in ways that clearly demarcate who is a Christian and who is not. So, for instance, we may define a Christian in terms of particular beliefs (creedal orthodoxy) or particular practices. For example, a person who believes in the virgin birth, substitutionary atonement, the deity of Christ, and who doesn't cuss, smoke, or drink: that person is a Christian. Others who do not share those beliefs and practices are not.

In a relational-set dominant culture, however, the category of Christian will be determined based on whom the person is primarily relating with. Are they following Jesus? Do they worship and serve him? In this view, Hiebert notes that we are able to appreciate that at least two stages

72. Hiebert, *Transforming Worldviews*, 34–36.

are involved in transformation. The first stage is that of rejecting our old gods, turning around, and choosing to follow Jesus. The second stage is our moving closer to Jesus throughout a lifetime of serving, learning, and worshipping.[73]

Hiebert notes that people who think in terms of intrinsic-set categories are often uncomfortable with relational-set category formation because it is more difficult to discern who is a Christian and who is not. This leads to the next topic.

Digital (Well-Formed) Sets versus Ratio (Fuzzy) Sets

Digital sets refer to category formation based on "clearly delineated . . . sets with a finite number of categories in a domain."[74] There is absolute clarity concerning who belongs to a category and who does not. I am either male or female. I am either fifty years old and under or above fifty. I am either Caucasian or some other clearly delineated ethnicity. There is no in-between.

Ratio sets (also described as *analogical*), however, are much less clear. These "fuzzy" sets are quite uncomfortable for persons whose worldview executes category formation using digital sets. The Western musician, for example, accustomed to seven notes and five half notes (no more and no less) finds Indian music to be strange indeed, for not only are there sixty-four steps between the C and the D on the classical scale, but the musician may subdivide even further if he or she so desires.[75] The same discomfort is experienced as digital-set Christians try to conceive of conversion in fuzzy-set terms. Digital-set Christians prefer to say that a person is either a Christian or they are not. "There is no middle ground!"[76] Ratio-set Christians, however, may query how realistic this perspective is regarding a Hindu who is considering a life of following Christ and has begun making steps in that direction, but is not yet ready to forsake everything that being a Hindu

73. Hiebert, *Transforming Worldviews*, 308–9.

74. Ibid., 33.

75. Ibid., 33–34.

76. I have sometimes heard Revelation 3:14–16 used to substantiate this perspective: "And to the angel of the church in Laodicea write: 'The words of the Amen, the faithful and true witness, the beginning of God's creation. I know your works: you are neither cold nor hot. Would that you were either cold or hot! So, because you are lukewarm, and neither hot nor cold, I will spit you out of my mouth.'"

implies for him or her. Could we not conceive of them as being part Hindu and part Christian until they become fully Christian? Hiebert admits that this raises difficult theological questions. But he also wonders if it might be "that what appears fuzzy to us, because we cannot see into the heart, is clear to God."[77]

Biblical View of Transformation

Hiebert proposes that the biblical view of transformation is better understood in terms of relational sets as they more accurately portray the Hebraic thought underlying much of the Bible. "The emphasis is not on what things are in themselves but on what things are in relationship to other things and to history."[78] In U.S. America our tendency is to think in terms of intrinsic sets, with a consequent stress on right beliefs and right practices. Hiebert does not suggest that right beliefs and right practices are unimportant, but he does point out that the Protestant clarion call of "salvation by faith, not by works" is quite inconsistent with an intrinsic-set insistence on what *we* believe and what *we* do, as opposed to the biblical understanding that transformation is "first and foremost the work of God."[79] Hiebert also contends that biblical worldview transformation is better served through a fuzzy-set perspective than a digital-set perspective, for this allows us to think more in terms of conversion as a process (as discussed above). Combining the two (the relational-set emphasis with the fuzzy-set emphasis), Hiebert writes that "conversion then is a point—a turning around. This turning may involve a minimal amount of information regarding Christ, but it does involve a change in relationship to him—a commitment to follow him, however little we know of him, to learn more and to obey him as we understand his voice. But conversion is also a process—a series of decisions that grow out of this initial turning."[80] This view of conversion highlights the need for evangelism and discipleship to be closely linked, and it reminds us that neither evangelism nor discipleship should be divorced from the church.[81]

77. Hiebert, *Transforming Worldviews*, 309.
78. Ibid., 310.
79. Ibid.
80. Ibid., 311.
81. Ibid., 312.

Implications for Evangelism

Hiebert believes that his proposal carries important implications for evangelism. If we view transformation (conversion) from the perspective of both relational and fuzzy sets, we will see that it means "to turn away (*shub*) from idols and to make Christ the central relationship in our lives."[82] From our perspective, the category of Christian may be fuzzy because we cannot see the heart. From God's perspective, however, the category is quite clear (digital), because God does see the heart. The most important test, therefore, is not what a person believes or does, but rather whom they follow as Lord.[83] Some new Christians may have scant knowledge of Jesus and his ways, and therefore do not really know what they should believe—much less what they do believe—but they are seeking him with integrity and passion. Some people who have been following Christ for much longer may have more knowledge concerning what they believe, but they still live mostly for themselves. The role of evangelism, therefore, "is not to determine who is in and who is out, but to encourage everyone, nonbeliever and believer alike, to become a totally committed follower of Christ and to grow in relationship with him."[84]

Eight Significant Themes

Based on the exploration of Barth, Moltmann, Oden, Kelsey, Anderson, and Hiebert, the following eight themes are particularly significant for life-based evangelism:

- Our experience of life must be linked to our relationship with and commitment to God who is the source and giver of life.

- Life as God intends is relational and communal.

- God intends that the life that God gives through Jesus and the Spirit will impact all spheres and dimensions of life (such as personal, familial, communal, relational, social, economic, political, and cultural).

- God desires holistic flourishing for us.

---

82. Hiebert, *Transforming Worldviews*, 282.
83. Ibid., 292.
84. Ibid.

- The life of holistic flourishing that God intends will include a biblically appropriate understanding and experience of joy, delight, or happiness.

- Life is God's ultimate goal for God's creation and God's creatures.

- There is a balance or tension between life-now and life-then.

- Life as God intends cannot be divorced from God's created material world.

  We turn in the next chapter to a brief treatment of each theme.

6

Eight Important Themes

Our Experience of Life Must Be Linked to Our Relationship with and Commitment to God

THE THEME THAT OUR experience of life must be linked to our relationship with and commitment to God is one of Barth's major contributions to a theological understanding of life. As stated earlier, although this may seem to be a simple point, it is yet a vital one. It helps us remember that although we want to help people understand and embrace the fullness of life that Jesus offers them, in the final analysis we are not inviting them to a what (life) but to a who (Jesus).

The link between our experience of life and our relationship with God was also clearly seen in the biblical studies material. Related to the Old Testament, for example, I referred to the way in which both Otto Baab and Edmund Jacob observe that human beings are "contingent" upon God, so that outside our relationship with God we are not fully human. Similarly, in the treatment of Johannine theology (chapter 4), we discovered John's robust stress on the call to believe, know, abide with, and obey Jesus. It would be impossible for John to conceive of a person experiencing life as God intends outside of or separate from a relationship with Jesus.

Given the U.S. American context of this project, I must briefly address the U.S. American tendency to view God as something or someone other than the Creator and Sovereign to whom we would appropriately give our first (and utmost) loyalty, commitment, and love. There is a sharp tendency among U.S. Americans (Christians and non-Christians alike) to allow their passion for the ideals of freedom, capitalism, and so on, to blind them to the biblical call to worship God and God alone. Leslie Newbigin observes that the question each person must address is: "am I living in total faithfulness, trust and loving obedience to him who is the sovereign?"[1] Douglas Harink as influenced by Stanley Hauerwas suggests that the primary dilemma in U.S. American churches is divided loyalties. Whether a church is theologically liberal or conservative seems not to matter. Most churches (and presumably, therefore, the Christians who attend those churches) are "divided between allegiance to American liberal democracy and society on the one hand and to the triune God revealed in Jesus Christ on the other."[2]

Idolatry or divided loyalties will resurface as we discuss subsequent themes. For the moment the essential point is that evangelistic theory and practice in the United States must pay attention to the strong tendency for U.S. Americans to compartmentalize any religious or spiritual experience as part of their religious or spiritual life (as opposed to their life as a whole), to the extent that it has little impact in other arenas. In this manner, therefore, though in church they may worship God and God alone (or at least think they are doing so), in other dimensions of their lives God is not allowed place or influence. How, therefore, can we portray (and invite persons to) an experience of full life in Jesus that appropriately calls them to center that experience in their commitment to and relationship with God?

Life as God Intends Is Relational and Communal

There are two dimensions of the theme "life as God intends is relational and communal" that are distinct yet interwoven. One has to do with God's intent that human beings relate with one another in their experience of the life for which God created them, now made possible through Jesus. The other has to do with God's intent that Christ-followers form a new people or community or society that would in turn be the primary agent of God's work in the world.

We Are to Relate with One Another in the Life God Intends

One of my consistent claims in this book is that full life in Christ cannot be experienced, expressed, or shared outside the scope of relationships. This claim receives clear support from Barth, Moltmann, Kelsey, Anderson, and Hiebert, all of whom strongly emphasize the relational nature of God, human

1. Newbigin, *Sign of the Kingdom*, 35.
2. Harink, *Paul Among the Postliberals*, 84.

beings, and the community of those who follow Jesus. Moreover, it was supported in the Johannine chapter (chapter 4), based in particular upon the shepherding imagery in John 10, the "love one another" command in John 13, and the "that they may all be one" phrase in Jesus's prayer in John 17.

I also briefly mentioned John Wesley's view of Christianity as being social in nature. Howard Snyder's view as influenced by Wesley makes a good starting place for us to now address this issue more fully. Snyder recommends that Wesley's emphasis upon the social nature of Christianity was based on his theological recognition that human beings are created in the image of God, and that one aspect of God's image is the relational (social for Wesley) interplay within the persons of the Trinity. It is part of God's very nature to be relational, and it is thus part of our very nature too.[3] The point to emphasize here is that our relational nature is not simply based on who God created us to be, but also on who God is.

Miguel A. de la Torre is another theologian who argues against our efforts to privatize the experience of full life in Christ. He contends that our relationship with Jesus, though personal and intimate, is never private. In fact, he further contends that "confining Jesus to my personal life becomes the ultimate act of religious selfishness."[4] Colson and Harold also spotlight what they refer to as "the myth of personal autonomy" and suggest that to think of our lives as belonging to us is pure folly. "Believing we are independent is simply a fiction—an increasingly unhelpful one. We all live in a vast network of friends, family, coworkers, and the incredibly complex associations that make up a culture. . . . The good life is found only in loving relationships and community."[5] Art McPhee agrees with this position. Building on D. T. Niles's description of evangelism's purpose as the recovery of wholeness, McPhee maintains that in addition to leading persons back to God, the ministry of evangelism should also lead them to God's people, "for community is a vital part of wholeness too."[6] As with other themes we have encountered, the key here seems to be learning how to embrace and communicate the dynamic tension involved in the need and invitation to personally respond to and relate with Jesus along with the need

3. Snyder, *Yes in Christ*, 20.

4. de la Torre, *Reading the Bible from the Margins*, 136-7.

5. Colson and Fickett, *Good Life*, 112–20.

6. McPhee, *Friendship Evangelism*, 111.

and invitation to do so within an already existing social network, as well as within a new social network of fellow Christ-followers.[7]

God's New People: Becoming God's New Society or Community in the World

The first dimension of the theme of becoming God's new people has to do with the fact that the individual Christ-follower cannot experience the full life that Jesus intends for him or her outside of relational community. The second dimension has to do with the fact that there is more at stake here than the impact that Christ-following has in my own experience of full life in Jesus. What is also at stake is that the primary agent God wants to use to bring full life to others is the new community that is formed by those who follow Jesus. This has been a passionate theme of many scholars in recent decades, several of whom build on John Yoder's work. Bryan Stone is one such person. He urges an understanding of evangelism that grows out of the social, public, embodied witness of the people of God. He suggests that the influence of Constantinian assumptions and Enlightenment philosophy has caused evangelism to be unduly conceived of in terms of winning individual persons to a personal relationship with Christ. In this evangelism, both the individual's relationship with Christ and the practice of evangelism are divorced from the church, with a primary focus on individual piety rather than the public witness of the ecclesia. In contrast, Stone maintains that the practice of evangelism should be based on an understanding of the church's politic (a new alternative public) and the church's economics

7. In chapter 1 made a brief reference to Claude Fischer's proposal that voluntarism is the predominant cultural reality in the United States. His conception of voluntarism is germane at this point. He agrees with other scholars that individualism is an extremely powerful characteristic of U.S. American culture, but he suggests that we should nuance our understanding regarding individualism to include reference to the participation in groups which is also a prevalent facet of the U.S. American scene. Voluntarism, therefore, consists of two primary elements. The first is "believing and behaving *as if* each person is a sovereign individual," and the second is "believing and behaving *as if* individuals succeed through fellowship . . . in sustaining, voluntary communities" (Fischer, *Made in America*, 10). If Fischer is correct, there is a built-in understanding among U.S. Americans concerning how to value both individualism and participation in groups, and this is germane to the current discussion. A point to be aware of, however, is that in voluntarism, the participation in groups is for the purpose of succeeding as individuals, so though the notion of social and relational participation is present among U.S. American believers and non-believers alike, this notion may be unconsciously driven by self-serving interests.

(a transformed *oikos*).[8] Furthermore, Stone suggests that participation in this social and public life together as God's people is what constitutes the essence of salvation. "These new patterns of kinship and social relation are not merely an *implication* of one's prior acceptance of salvation. Rather, they are precisely that which is offered *as* salvation."[9] Thus, Stone argues against the type of evangelism that seeks first to convince persons to accept a personal relationship with Christ and then subsequently encourages them to participate in the social and public embodiment of Christ's peaceable reign. He maintains that participation in the social and public embodiment of Christ's peaceable reign through God's people (the church) is part and parcel of conversion, not subsequent to it.[10]

Jim Wallis also calls for a social and communal understanding of life in Christ and advocates that there is a vital connection between this understanding and our influence in the world. The early Christ-followers lived in community with one another and patterned their lives after Jesus's teachings, including those in the Sermon on the Mount.[11] The result was that "they became well known as a caring, sharing, and open community that was especially sensitive to the poor and the outcast."[12] Wallis indicates that this is more than a simple awareness on the part of the world that individual Christians were well known for these things. Instead, "a new human society" had arisen, in which "love was given daily expression." For Wallis, therefore, it is not simply that this new human society now shares the gospel. It is rather that "the existence of the church itself, that inclusive community that knows no human boundaries, becomes a part of the good news."[13] Dallas Willard agrees with this emphasis on the new society that is called out and formed by God, and he even submits that this was included in God's plan for creation from the very beginning.[14]

Other examples could be proffered of theologians who agree with the general idea that at least one of God's primary interests in the world is to create a new people, community, body-politic, or society from those who

---

8. Stone, *Evangelism after Christendom*, 177–204.

9. Ibid., 78.

10. Ibid., 10–17. (We hear strong echoes here of Ray Anderson's theory that Christian community provides the fundamental liturgical paradigm for authentic personhood.)

11. Wallis, *Call to Conversion*, 8–17.

12. Ibid., 15.

13. Ibid., 117. See also 15–19 and 111–37.

14. Willard, *Divine Conspiracy*, 385–6.

choose to follow Christ, and that this new body is the foremost instrument God wants to use to help all of God's creation know God and be known by God, and in so doing experience the kind of life that God intended from the beginning. The related issue that pertains to this project is at least twofold:

- How accurate is the general idea concerning a body-politic?
- Should it be included in evangelistic theory and practice?

Is it that the Christian community is where people best find their way toward choosing to follow Jesus? Is it that through participation in the Christian community they have actually already made that choice? Is it something that combines the two?

I believe that a combination of the two is the most helpful way to conceive of this issue, but with a stronger emphasis on the notion that it is in the Christian community where people often find their way toward choosing to follow Jesus. To maintain a heavier emphasis on the idea that through participation in the Christian community a person has therefore chosen to follow Jesus is dangerous in at least two ways. First, it blurs the clear distinction between following the person of Jesus and being a part of the worldwide fellowship of those who are also following him. Second, it potentially diminishes the crucial importance of the need that each individual has to make a personal decision to follow him. This decision is to be made within the context of relationships with other people, so that it is not privatized. But although it is not a privatized decision, it must yet be a personal one.

God Intends that Full Life in Jesus Will Impact All Spheres or Dimensions of Life

The assertion that God intends that full life in Jesus will impact all spheres of life has strong support among a large number of theologians. We recall that Moltmann highlights this theme along two lines. First he notes that life in the Spirit is not to be limited to the new community of the exodus, but rather is to be shared with persons outside that community. Second, he refers to the three world processes that the new community of the exodus must impact: economic, political, and cultural.

Hiebert's approach is very different from Moltmann's, but he also argues for comprehensive impact. He proposes that Christ-centered transformation must involve all three primary dimensions of culture (cognitive, affective, and evaluative) and that the transformation should work deeply enough to change our underlying worldview.

Moltmann and Hiebert are certainly not the lone proponents of the all-dimensions impact that is envisioned when we follow Jesus. We have already observed that a large number of scholars argue against the privatization and individualization of Christian experience. An evident corollary would seem to easily follow: if Christian experience is not to be privatized and individualized, then it certainly must be intended to impact all spheres of life. I believe, however, that there is yet a need to address this as a separate theme. During my 25 years of pastoral ministry, I have observed that there are some Christians in the United States who may acknowledge the need to be in relationship with other Christians as they journey through life, but their primary objective in these relationships is to help them grow in *their* relationship with Jesus. In other words, they recognize that they should not privatize their Christ-following experience, but their "sharing" or "flowering" of that experience still primarily impacts them and their small circle of friends. It has little or no influence in the larger world around them. Rather than allowing God's values to change their perspectives on politics, economics, justice, peace, creation care, and much more, they "baptize" their already-existent beliefs concerning those issues in the name of Christianity. Therefore, though much in their lives may have changed as a result of following Christ, few if any of those changes are evident outside their relational network.

In his development of an ecclesiology for integral mission, Rene Padilla points out that evangelical Christians stress the title *Savior* when referring to Jesus, though the title *Lord* (*kyrios* in Greek) is used far more often in the New Testament. He notes that not only is *kyrios* the word used to translate the Hebrew YHWH (Yahweh), but it is also the title used to refer to the Roman emperor in the first century. For the early Christians to call Jesus *Kyrios*, therefore, suggests "recognition of his sovereignty over the whole of human life and over the whole creation." In this context, then, Padilla proposes that "the call of the gospel is a call to a total transformation that reflects God's purpose to redeem human life in all its dimensions."[15] Based on a similar emphasis on God's sovereignty, Leslie Newbigin proposes that Christ-followers are called to be a "sign, instrument, and foretaste" of God's sovereignty in all of life.[16] He encourages us to avoid the

---

15. Padilla, "Introduction: An Ecclesiology for Integral Mission," 19–49.

16. Newbigin, *Foolishness to the Greeks*, 124.

two primary temptations that face Christ-followers: to blend church and culture together as happened in western Europe for a millennium, or to relegate their Christian experience to a private sector that has no bearing on "the ideology that rules the public life of nations."[17] A crucial part of our experience of full life in Jesus is to be the "signs and agents of God's justice in all human affairs. An evangelism that invites men and women to accept the name of Christ but fails to call them to this real encounter must be rejected as false."[18] Nothing is to remain outside God's purview.

One of the impressive and intriguing features of John Wesley's life and theology is how interested he was in a wide range of issues and topics. In addition to his focus on embodying Christ's love through ministries in prisons, factories, coal mines, and so on, he also was involved in a great number of what some would call "secular" pursuits. Snyder refers to this as the "comprehensiveness" of "the Wesleyan lens." He writes that "in his day, very little escaped John Wesley's notice—from the 'improvement' of the land in the Scottish Highlands, to the working conditions of the coal miners, to the workings of the Spirit in a child's life, to new discoveries about the circulation of the blood. And he reflected biblically and theologically on everything."[19]

It is Wesley's biblical and theological reflection on everything that should be highlighted for the current discussion. If our experience of full life in Jesus is going to truly impact and involve all spheres or dimensions of our lives, both personally and publically, then we must avoid the temptation to limit our biblical and theological reflection only to the "sacred" dimensions of our lives. Every dimension of our lives merits such reflection (plus action and application), because Jesus's intention is to transform and/or impact every dimension of people's individual lives as well as every dimension of their corporate, public, cultural, political, and economic lives.

The dilemma with which to struggle, therefore, is how evangelism can seek to avoid situations in which persons make an initial decision to follow Christ based on a lack of understanding of, appreciation for, and commitment to, the all-dimensions impact that following Jesus is intended to have in our lives.

17. Newbigin, *Foolishness to the Greeks*, 124–5.
18. Ibid., 133.
19. Snyder, *Yes in Christ*, 16.

God Desires Holistic Flourishing for Us

You may already recognize that God desires that all of God's creation—including human beings—flourish holistically based on what I've shared so far, but it is worthwhile to again confirm the significance of this point. I submit that God's intent is that we experience life that is full and vital, not life that is half-empty and filled with constant struggles. As has been said before, this does not mean that life will be free of suffering or problems, but the general experience of life in Jesus, even in the midst of suffering and problems, is intended to be that of holistic flourishing. God's creation was (and is) good, and the life God intends for us in Jesus is good too. To reinforce this affirmation we will take a brief sojourn into Germain Grisez's conception of integral communal fulfillment. He suggests that the true ultimate end of human beings (that toward which we should direct our lives) is "integral communal fulfillment in God's kingdom, which will be a marvelous communion of divine Persons, human persons, and other created persons." This integral communal fulfillment will include the beatific vision, but it will also include "every human member of the kingdom" being "richly fulfilled . . . in respect to all the fundamental human goods."[20]

Especially germane is Grisez's insistence that "our ultimate end must include our own well-being and flourishing," and his subsequent claim that this concept of well-being must include "the fundamental goods of human beings."[21] These "goods" include life, health, bodily integrity, skillful work, play, and harmony (with God, others, and self).[22] Of special import is his assumption that a life of well-being and flourishing is not an idealized vision that is beyond us. To the contrary, through the gifts of divine revelation, Jesus, and the Holy Spirit, God "enables those who believe in Jesus to cooperate with Him by discerning and carrying out God's plan for their lives."[23] A life of holistic flourishing is not only God's intention for us; through Jesus it is God's possibility for us.

20. Grisez, "True Ultimate End of Human Beings," 58–59.
21. Ibid., 54.
22. Ibid.
23. Ibid., 57–58.

Life as God Intends Includes a Biblically Appropriate Experience of Joy, Delight, or Happiness

Biblically, there is no questioning the strong link between joy and the lives we live in Jesus. In the New Testament, this begins even before Jesus's birth, as seen in the angel's proclamation to the shepherds ("Fear not, for behold, I bring you good news of great joy that will be for all the people"), and it continues throughout the New Testament.[24] In John 15 Jesus says, "These things I have spoken to you, that my joy may be in you, and that your joy may be full."[25] In Romans 14 Paul writes that "the kingdom of God is not a matter of eating and drinking but of righteousness and peace and joy in the Holy Spirit."[26] In Galatians 5:22 we learn that joy is a fruit of the Holy Spirit, and in 1 Peter we read Peter's confirmation to diaspora Christians that "though you do not now see him, you believe in him and rejoice with joy that is inexpressible and filled with glory."[27]

The Old Testament also refers often to joy. The psalmist declares to the Lord that "you make known to me the path of life; in your presence there is fullness of joy."[28] Isaiah prophesies that "the ransomed of the Lord shall return and come to Zion with singing; everlasting joy shall be upon their heads; they shall obtain gladness and joy, and sorrow and sighing shall flee away."[29]

Importantly, this is not a joy that we only experience during the good times in our lives. Barth and others affirm that the fact that Jesus suffered a painful death on the cross, along with other biblical instruction, teaches us that joy is dependent more on our relationship with and trust in God than on our circumstances at any particular time. Thus it is that Habakkuk can say: "Though the fig tree should not blossom, nor fruit be on the vines, the produce of the olive fail and the fields yield no food, the flock be cut off from the fold and there be no herd in the stalls, yet I will rejoice in the Lord; I will take joy in the God of my salvation."[30]

24. Luke 2:10.
25. John 15:11.
26. Rom 14:17.
27. 1 Pet 1:8.
28. Ps 16:11.
29. Isa 51:11.
30. Hab 3:17–18.

Joy, happiness, and delight are portrayed in the Bible as expected elements of life when lived with and in God. This was a deep-seated belief of John Wesley too. Some people find it hard to discern this Wesleyan emphasis in the midst of his talk about duty and discipline, but Albert Outler suggests that the Christian disciplines Wesley advocated had as their goal the blessedness and happiness of the Christ-follower. He proposes that Wesley focused on Christian duty and discipline in order to help persons avoid seeking happiness in places where it could not be found. It is only in and with God that we can be truly blessed and happy, so when we discipline ourselves to seek God and God's ways instead of placing our hope for happiness in other things, we find that we move much closer to that blessed state. Happiness for Wesley, therefore, was an integral dimension of God's intentions for all people.[31]

John Schneider's work is helpful in examining the role of joy, delight, and happiness in Christian living. He suggests that we must have a fuller comprehension of the "cosmic vision of delight" that is portrayed in the book of Genesis. This cosmic vision of delight means not only that it is good to experience joy, delight, and happiness in our Christian lives, but even more importantly, that it is paradigmatic. It describes for us what God's intention is for all people, and "it is therefore the frame of reference for the sort of vision that Christians ought to have for humanity in the here and now."[32] For Schneider this perspective is strongly confirmed by close observation of Jesus in the Gospels. There are two portrayals of Jesus in the Gospel narratives. One is a radical Jesus who requires a severance of previous relationships and virtual poverty. The other, however, is the Lord of Delight who celebrates life so passionately that the religious authorities were offended and shocked. In this portrayal, Jesus "brought the warmth of new life—freedom, camaraderie, peace, good cheer, and a mood of joyous celebration."[33]

Timothy Keller shares a similar perspective. He likens the experience of salvation to a great experiential feast. We not only believe that Jesus loves us, but "we can come to sense the reality, the beauty, and the power of his love," and we learn that Jesus's love "can delight, galvanize, and console you." Keller refers to this as "festival joy."[34]

31. Outler, *Evangelism and Theology in the Wesleyan Spirit*, 128.

32. Schneider, *Good of Affluence*, 41–45.

33. Ibid., 139–41.

34. Keller, *Prodigal God*, 106–9.

The ministry of evangelism must consider how to address the issue of joy, delight, or happiness. It is too prevalent in the biblical material and too important in theological reflection to simply ignore it in evangelism.

Life Is God's Ultimate Goal

This has already been dealt with in chapter 2, where I made a distinction between life as the goal and the kingdom as one of the instruments or means to reach that goal (or as the arena in which that goal was fulfilled). This topic was also treated in the Johannine chapter (chapter 4), where the "so that" references in John's Gospel were highlighted in order to provide additional biblical warrant for seeing life as God's ultimate goal. Additionally, we noted in chapter 5 that both Moltmann and Oden see life as the central outcome that God intends in Jesus. Thus, sufficient evidence has been provided to confirm that life is at the very least a principal biblical and theological theme, and that it should therefore be reflected in evangelistic theory and practice.

The Balance or Tension between Life-Now and Life-Then

Accepting the balance or tension between life-now and life-then is another theme that we discussed previously. Two points in particular bear recalling. First is that the reason we experience tension between life-now and life-then is that we are living in the overlap between the present age and the age to come. We cannot (and should not) do away with the tension between these two ages. Too many Christians mistakenly assume that the tension is between a fully powerful-and-present old age and a partially powerful-and-present age to come. The new age (the age to come), however, has come in its fullness. We have already received the possibility of new life in Christ in full measure. The reason we sometimes do not yet experience the full measure of this new life is that we live in the overlap between the old age and the age to come; thus, the complete destruction of the old age has not yet taken place. It is not that we live in some third age in which the fullness of life is weaker than it will be in the age to come. Rather, it is that the old age continues to exert its influence and power.

The second point has to do with the symbiotic relationship between life-now and life-then. Our trust that there is yet something even greater awaiting us after our physical death gives us a different lens through which to view our lives now. This in turn helps us experience a fuller life now because we have the faith perspective of the full blessings of the age to come.

We should not, therefore, do away with the tension between life-now and life-then, but evangelistic theory and practice should more fully address the life-now side of this tension. This issue has been more than adequately treated throughout this project, but I nevertheless would like to introduce Dallas Willard's thoughts about it, for he has a viewpoint that speaks forcefully to this issue's role in evangelism.

Willard observes that the versions of the "gospel" that tend to be communicated concerning full life in Jesus are shaped in one of two ways. First is the focus on preparing for what will happen after we die, and the second is to get involved in improving social practices and conditions. Willard agrees that both of these emphases are essential, but he likewise argues that "neither one touches the quick of individual existence or taps the depths of the reality of Christ. . . . Does Jesus only enable me to 'make the cut' when I die? Or to know what to protest, or how to vote or agitate and organize? It is good to know that when I die all will be well, but is there any good news for life? If I had to choose, I would rather have a car that runs than good insurance on one that doesn't. Can I not have both?"[35] I submit that many non-believers in the United States are asking Willard's question, is there any good news for life? The answer is, yes, there is very good news for life now, and evangelistic theory and practice must make this a primary emphasis.

Life as God Intends Cannot Be Divorced from God's Created Material World

We cannot divorce life as God intends from God's created material world. This theme will be discussed in two parts. The first has to do with the role of creation care, and the second has to do with the materiality of the human experience of full life in Jesus.

The Concept of Full Life and the Entire Creation

In *The Source of Life*, Moltmann writes about the "three waves" of the mission of the Holy Spirit. The first wave is the renewal of God's people. The second is the renewal of all living things. The third is the renewal of

---

35. Willard, *Divine Conspiracy*, 12.

the face of the earth. Moltmann argues that the earth should not be seen as distinct from and less sacred than human persons, but rather as a fellow member of God's comprehensive created order that is being renewed in Jesus.[36] In the context of Revelation 21, which talks of a new heaven and a new earth, he proposes that "there is no eternal life without the kingdom of God, and no kingdom of God without the new earth."[37] Howard Snyder echoes these sentiments. He contends that the healing of creation is part and parcel of God's overall redemptive plan, not secondary to it. "Scripture presents salvation as an immense divine plan for the redemption of all creation, 'the restoration of all things' (Acts 3:21). We read in Ephesians 1:10 that God has a plan (*oikonomia*) for the fullness of time to bring everything in heaven and earth together in reconciliation under the headship of Jesus Christ—*all things*, things in heaven and things on earth; things visible and invisible. The plan of redemption is as broad as the scope of creation and the depth of sin."[38]

Matthew Sleeth also encourages a strong connection between creation care and Christian living.[39] He has done extensive work in surveying biblical references to parts of God's creation. Based on this work, he demonstrates that the Bible is filled with references to God's material creation, and notes that many of these references are intentionally linked with God's purposes in the world. Consider trees, for example. A tree plays an important role in the early stages of the Bible (Genesis 3), and also in the last chapter of the Bible (Revelation 22, the tree of life). Moreover, the very centerpiece of Christian theology, the crucifixion, takes place on a tree. Additionally, we are reminded that trees are our source of oxygen, so that without them we literally would be unable to live.[40] Also important to Sleeth's theology is the translation of the Hebrew in Genesis 2:15, which he suggests should read that we are to "protect and serve" the earth.[41] It is the call to protect and serve the earth that helps him envision his life with Christ as including creation care. Therefore,

36. Moltmann, *Source of Life*, 22–25.

37. Ibid., 25.

38. Snyder, "Salvation Means Creation Healed," 11.

39. Sleeth, "Power of a Green God," 117–124.

40. Ibid., 120–21.

41. Ibid., 122. This verse states that God placed "the man" in the garden of Eden "to protect and serve it" (according to Sleeth). For comparison purposes, the ESV translates this phrase as "to work it and keep it."

rather than thinking of creation care as ancillary to full life in Jesus, he says that it "is at the very core" of our journey with Jesus.[42]

There is no question that creation care should be an integral part of our experience of full life in Jesus, but what part should it play in the theory and practice of evangelism? This is the pressing question. I mentioned earlier that although evangelism cannot deliver everything that is involved in full life in Christ, it nevertheless should portray a complete picture of that full life in Christ on the front end, so that persons who choose to follow Christ will know what they are being asked to embrace. Following that suggestion, therefore, we would want to find a way to include creation care in at least some versions of the essential gospel message. A potential dilemma at this point, however, revolves around the fear that if we include everything that God intends in the full life God wants to give, we will be shaping a gospel message that is overly complex and burdensome. Is there a way to include creation care in evangelistic theory and practice that does not do this? I will address this further in chapter 8.

The Materiality of the Human Experience of Full Life in Jesus

David Kelsey accentuates this theme of the materiality of the human experience of full life in Jesus in the aforementioned material concerning the provisional nature of our lives as lived in the finite quotidian (chapter 5). This reminds us that the life Jesus intends is not a "spiritual experience" disconnected from who we are as "personal living bodies," nor is it detached from the finite and real world in which we live. To further address this topic, we return to Schneider's cosmic vision of delight. Schneider proposes that not only is it vital to grasp the paradigmatic value of Genesis's cosmic vision of delight, but it is equally important to understand that God's vision of delight is a material one.[43] The creation story depicts life that is teeming, fertile, and abundant. Yes, we are spiritual beings, but we are also material beings, rational beings, moral beings, and much more. Our bodies are an essential part of who we are, and given God's declaration of God's physical creation as very good, Schneider suggests that rather than moving too quickly to thinking of physical and material pleasure and joy in terms of hedonistic excess, we should first think of them as expressions of "deep

---

42. Sleeth, "Power of a Green God," 121.

43. Schneider, *Good of Affluence*, 43.

godliness and humanness."[44] There are certainly inappropriate excesses that must be avoided, but Schneider believes that we jump too quickly to that type of judgment. This causes us to miss the crucial point that we were created to enjoy our lives in and with God's created material world. Just as God delighted in God's own creation, pronouncing it good, so too God delights in our delight.[45]

Schneider provides us with a good segue into a topic that warrants discussion due to the influence of the prosperity gospel in the United States: How does financial wealth factor into our experience of full life in Jesus? Schneider contends that the materiality of God's cosmic vision of delight includes the enjoyment of financial wealth.[46] Christian teaching regarding wealth has tended to be negative, but Schneider argues that a narrative interpretation of Scripture that includes a sharp grasp of the historical and cultural contexts from which most of the anti-wealth biblical passages have arisen will help us see that it is not primarily wealth in and of itself that God opposes, but rather the acquisition of wealth through oppression of others. This is particularly true of the prophetic tradition. Schneider claims that we must recognize that the prophets did not speak against wealth per se, but spoke rather against the king and the ruling classes who had achieved wealth at the expense of the people for whose economic welfare they were responsible. The historical and cultural context of the prophetic tradition is nothing like the situation in which most ordinary Western Christians find themselves today.[47] Therefore, to apply the prophetic judgment to them that was directed against the kings and ruling classes during the time of the prophets "is perilously unfair."[48]

Far from being evil, therefore, Schneider views material prosperity as an essential dimension of God's cosmic vision of delight. He writes that "it is a fundamental biblical theme that material prosperity (rightly understood) is the condition that God envisions for all human beings when he creates the world. It describes the condition that God has in view for human beings in eternity. And it describes the condition that God (circumstances being

44. Schneider, *Good of Affluence*, 58.

45. Ibid., 58–61.

46. Ibid., 154–60.

47. Ibid., 91–98.

48. Ibid., 97. Bear in mind here the references I made in chapter 2 to the role of kings in the Ancient Near East to provide a secure and just environment for the enjoyment of prosperous well-being.

right) desires for human beings now."[49] He points to Mercedes-Benz automobiles as an example. These cars are carefully designed and finely crafted, and their creators and builders must certainly reap immense fulfillment and pleasure, as do those who drive them. Why should we assume that owning such a vehicle is inappropriate for those who follow Jesus? Schneider contends that other than simple resentment, there is no reason to think of this kind of material pleasure as unhealthy materialism. To the contrary, "why not instead wish that everyone could enjoy life at those levels?" He agrees that there is a temptation to corrupt the God-intended desire for us to enjoy material things, but this does not preclude the possibility of enjoying material things in the right way.[50]

Schneider's view is tempered by scholars such as Ron Sider and Justo Gonzalez. Gonzalez suggests that Christian teaching throughout the centuries, though divergent at particular points, has consistently argued that: (a) the accumulation of wealth is inappropriate; (b) failing to provide financial assistance to someone when one has the ability to do so is sinful; (c) we should distinguish between the necessary and the superfluous, keeping only enough wealth to provide for our needs and sharing the rest with others; (d) private property exists because of our fallen condition (we must recognize God as the ultimate owner); and (e) the intended use of wealth is the common good.[51] Gonzalez's interpretation of pertinent New Testament passages leads him to emphasize economic koinonia as an essential dimension of the Christian community, which includes a total sharing among community members, both spiritual and material. This vision of economic koinonia is not based solely on the "all things in common" passages in the book of Acts. Reference is also made to Paul's stress on the Corinthian offering to benefit the Jerusalem church. Moreover, support for this view is found in 1 John 3:17–18, where John writes that if we see a fellow Christian in need and have resources to help, yet choose not to do so, God's love is not in us.[52]

Ron Sider spotlights the role of the poor in the biblical portrayal, noting that in the Old Testament God often acts on behalf of the poor and oppressed. Furthermore, Jesus invested a lot of time with the marginalized (lepers, despised women, hated tax collectors), "and he warned his followers

49. Schneider, *Good of Affluence*, 3.

50. Ibid., 37–39.

51. Gonzalez, *Faith and Wealth*, 225–9.

52. Ibid., 79–87.

in the strongest possible words that those who do not feed the hungry, clothe the naked, and visit the prisoners will experience eternal damnation (Matt 25:31–46)."[53] In addition to his strong emphasis on the poor and the biblical mandate to care for them, Sider advocates economic fellowship and economic justice. As with Gonzalez, Sider accentuates the koinonia of the early church. From its example we can glean two important insights: "First, God wants all people to have the productive resources to be able to earn a decent living and be dignified members of their community" and "Second, God wants the rest of us to provide a generous share of the necessities of life to those who cannot work."[54] The "community of the redeemed," should feature redeemed personal, social, and economic relationships.

Schneider applauds Sider's book overall as "a monument to good Christian social ethics," but he also feels that his argument is weak at two points. First is Sider's blanket application of the Old Testament prophetic message concerning economic evil then to Western Christians now. Schneider's hermeneutical case regarding this issue has already been outlined. The second place of weakness relates to Sider's claim that Christians with superfluous resources should give to those in need, and that failure to do so "is as important to faith and life as anything." Schneider contends that if Sider truly believes that economic sharing is essential to our being Christian, he should provide greater clarity regarding the standards or criteria by which we may discern what is necessary and what is superfluous. Instead of clarity, however, his writings leave an ambiguous portrayal.[55] "Sufficiency" seems to be the image that Sider and others finally recommend as the standard for discerning what is necessary and what is superfluous, and this is based in large part on Proverbs 30:8–9 ("give me neither poverty nor riches"). Schneider argues, however, that the creation and exodus narratives reveal that the exceeding of "arbitrary limits of 'sufficiency' or 'necessity'" is not the biblical standard for discerning whether a person has spiritual or moral integrity."[56] This perspective places far too much stress on one passage from the book of Proverbs. To the contrary, Schneider writes that "what makes affluence a cosmic good is just that it creates freedom for human beings

---

53. Sider, *Rich Christians in an Age of Hunger*, 41–47.

54. Ibid., 75–87.

55. Schneider, *Good of Affluence*, 92–103.

56. Ibid., 102–3.

and, in that light, that it makes possible the proper dominion, dignity, and delight which otherwise would be impossible."[57]

Grounded in his commitment to affluence as a cosmic good, Schneider proposes that the distinction that merits our attention is not between an appropriate enjoyment of wealth versus an extreme wealth that is thereby inappropriate. The more helpful contrast is "between extreme indulgence on the one hand and true delight on the other."[58] To support his view, he cites two allusions in Amos 6:4–7.[59] The first is the reference to King David. David was a man who enjoyed fine wines and good food; he danced and sang and played. David was "an archetype of delight, not evil." The second allusion is found in Amos's statement that the nation's leaders were not "grieved over the ruin of Joseph." This allusion reveals that the primary dilemma with the behavior of the leaders was not that they were eating and drinking, but that they were doing so in the midst of suffering all around them, and, moreover, they were oblivious to that suffering. "It is a matter of becoming a mature person with a vision from the Lord and a heart for people, especially the poor and powerless. The rich must be liberated not from riches but from the selfish mind and heart of the serpent."[60] The issue at stake, therefore, was that the leaders had lost touch with brokenness and were focused only on themselves.

How might one assess these varying perspectives regarding the place of wealth in Christian living, and what implications are at stake for the theory and practice of evangelism? Schneider's depiction of the cosmic vision of delight as an accurate portrayal of God's original intention in creation and God's intention for us now is to be affirmed. This honors the goodness of God's creation and the joy that we experience when we are in right relationship with God and others. It is also true that some measure of abundant provision is included in this cosmic vision. Given the stark differences between the historical, cultural, and economic settings from which the Bible emerged and the historical, cultural, and economic setting of the United States today, it would be extremely difficult to be precise concerning what that "some measure of abundant provision" should be, but there is no question that Scripture reveals multiple portrayals of abundant provision for those who are in right relationship with God. How much money is

57. Schneider, *Good of Affluence*, 103.
58. Ibid., 104.
59. Ibid., 105.
60. Ibid., 106.

enough? How much money is too much? Scholars like Gonzalez and Sider help us understand that we cannot aptly address those questions without considering our responsibility to share our wealth with those in economic need. Schneider agrees, but he comes at it from the perspective of "finding our true humanity," whereas Gonzalez and Sider address it from the perspective of the holistic koinonia that the community of the redeemed should embrace.

There is value in each perspective. One might say that Schneider's perspective more fully honors an anthropological view (what does it mean to be human as God intends?) whereas the perspective of Gonzalez and Sider more fully honors an ecclesiological view (what does it mean to be the redeemed people of God?).

The root of this issue lies in whether we are primarily focused on ourselves or on God and others. If our primary focus is on God, and we with integrity regularly seek God's guidance and wisdom concerning how to serve God and others, the Holy Spirit will direct our financial life. If the primary focus is on self, though, we will too easily fall into the trap of selfish accumulation and will have no regard for the economic plight of others. As we remain focused on God and others, it is both possible and appropriate to experience "abundant provision," but it is also crucial to remember that God's intention is that everyone experience full life in Jesus, which means that as God facilitates abundant provision for us, we want to use those resources to be channels of God's abundant provision for others. The use of *abundant provision* as the descriptor of choice avoids the use of *affluence* and the use of *prosperity. Affluence* may carry a built-in stigma for some persons, and *abundant* corresponds nicely with John 10:10. Concerning *prosperity,* it is too closely linked with the prosperity gospel.

There are two primary concerns with respect to the prosperity gospel. The first is that it too easily feeds the always-present human tendency toward selfishness, especially in the predominant U.S. American version of the prosperity gospel that emphasizes our "first-class nature" as "the King's Kids."[61] The comments concerning self-focus versus God-focus in the previous paragraph speak to this concern. The second concern with the prosperity gospel is a hermeneutical one. Most writers and preachers who advocate the prosperity gospel claim 3 John 1:2 as their foundational scriptural warrant. The King James Version is the translation most often used, and it says,

---

61. Recall the reference I made in chapter 1 to Gordon Fee's description of the prosperity gospel.

"Beloved, I wish above all things that thou mayest prosper and be in health, even as thy soul prospereth." The proponents of the prosperity gospel take the word *prosper* and make a universal application of that word to all Christians for all times. This is hermeneutically fallacious at two points. First, the Greek word is more accurately translated *go well with you,* and second, this is part of a standard greeting that was used in written salutations in that day and time. Essentially, then, the message was, "Dear Beloved, I hope all is well with you and that you are experiencing good health." To apply this as a universal affirmation that God wills all God's children to prosper financially is most inappropriate from a hermeneutical standpoint.[62]

The dilemma in critiquing the prosperity gospel is that it is difficult to distinguish between appropriate provision and inappropriate prosperity. Love for others is the important element here. If our hearts break for the things that break God's heart; if we have compassion for the people and causes for which God has compassion; then we will be sensitive to the needs of others and will count it a joy and privilege to generously share our resources with others. In so doing, we will help them experience abundant provision, and we will experience the gracious gift of partnering with God as an instrument of God's provision in their lives. Evangelistically, therefore, it is appropriate to invite persons to an experience of full life in Jesus, and it is further appropriate to communicate that this full life will include abundant material provision for their own lives along with the joyous opportunity to partner with God in providing for others.[63]

This concludes our exploration of theological insights regarding the biblical theme of life. We turn now to an analysis of the field research data, after which I will reflect on the insights from all three streams of research (biblical, theological, and field interviews) in order to discern the most important evangelistic implications of a strong focus on the biblical theme of life.

62. Fee, *Disease of the Health & Wealth Gospels,* 4.

63. I recognize that some persons may be specifically called to a life of poverty, but in the U.S. American context of my project, that would be more the exception than the rule.

7

What I Learned from Christ-Followers in Local Congregations

IN THIS CHAPTER, I will share what I learned from conversations with 153 persons in local congregations.[1] The following themes will be addressed:

- This-life versus next-life references

- Relational versus individual dynamics in the Christ-following journey

- The role of emotional well-being in responses from recent converts

- The belief that the life God intends for us should impact all dimensions of our lives

- The role of joy, delight, or happiness

- The consistency with which believers conceptualize the Christ-following journey in relation to how they relate with non-believers

1. I engaged in individual interviews with 111 of these people; the remaining forty-two were interviewed in small groups. The 153 persons were divided into four groups, based on input from the churches' pastors: recent converts, key influential leaders, evangelistically gifted leaders, and staff. This research took place in eight churches, six of which are United Methodist, one of which would be most accurately classified as evangelical Anglican, and one of which is a community church with a former evangelical United Methodist serving as pastor. These churches were selected based primarily on what Thom Rainer refers to as a "conversion ratio" (membership to annual conversions). Rainer suggests that an "effective evangelistic church" will have a ratio of less than 20:1, plus a minimum of twenty-six conversions per year (Rainer, *Surprising Insights from the Unchurched*, 23). Because I wanted to include some new churches in my research, I chose not to use the twenty-six conversions per year yardstick in the selection process, since some new churches begin relatively small and require a few years to gain sufficient momentum to reach that number. An additional factor I used in the selection process was the ratio of worship attendance to conversions, because worship attendance can serve as a good indicator of the current vitality of a congregation. Twenty-one questions were posed. There is not enough space for a complete report on all the questions. I will discuss only those that are most pertinent to the major themes of this project.

Tension or Continuum Regarding This-Life References and Next-Life References

One of the questions posed was as follows: In the Gospel of John, there are a lot of verses about life. In your experience and understanding, what does "life in Christ" mean? A thorough reading of the interview transcripts allowed me to group the responses into fourteen different categories. If a similar response was given a minimum of three times (representing 1 percent), then I assigned that response its own category. The response summary is portrayed in Table 4.1. Ten percent of the responses related to eternal life, which equals a ratio of nine this-life references to each next-life reference.

Table 4.1. Responses to the Question on the Meaning of Life in Christ (N=285)

Category	n	%
Emotional well-being	70	25
Fullness, abundance	50	18
Other	31	11
Eternal life	29	10
Loving/serving others	16	6
Relationship with or intimacy with God	15	5
Purpose/meaning/significance	14	5
Christ-likeness, fruit	15	5
Guidance, wisdom, direction	11	4
Big change/redemption	11	4
Discipleship, walk with Jesus	12	4
God with us, not alone	3	1
Forgiveness	4	1
Loved, accepted	4	1

Similar results emerge from the responses given to another question: Sometimes we refer to the "gospel" as "the good news." In your experience and/or understanding, what are some of the "good" dimensions of "the good news"? During my evaluation of these responses, I assigned separate categories to questions receiving a minimum of four responses. Eighteen categories emerged during this analysis, as portrayed in Table 4.2. We see in the table that references to eternity ranked in a tie for third place with two other categories of responses, and that the percentage of total responses was eight. One might also consider including other categories in this percentage, however, such as hope, forgiveness, and salvation/Jesus's sacrifice, since we might infer that these responses either emerge from a strong appreciation of eternal life or they point toward eternal life. I did not include them in the eternal life category because these responses did not include specific references to eternal life and I did not want to assume more than the respondents intended. However, to be fair to the eternal life end of the continuum, if we include these categories for the moment, the total percentage of next-life references is 21. This would make the next-life references the largest single category, but would still indicate that 79 percent of the responses envision the good dimensions of the good news in this-life terms, while 21 percent envision them in next-life terms (the ratio being 3.8 to 1).

Table 4.2. Responses to Participants' Understanding of the Good Dimensions of the Good News (N=222)

Category	n	%
Other	36	16
Guidance/how to live/better life	22	10
Eternity	19	8
Bible/the four Gospels	19	8
Love/compassion (of God)	19	8
Freedom	12	5
Peace/comfort/contentment/reassurance	12	5
Transform/heal/renew/restore/deliver	11	5
Never alone/God always with us	10	5
Grace/mercy	10	5
Salvation/Jesus's sacrifice	10	5
Forgiveness	9	4

Hope	8	4
Plan/meaning/purpose	7	3
Don't have to be perfect/acceptance	5	2
Relationship with God	5	2
Help in tough times	4	2
What's not good?/everything!	4	2

Another interview question that sheds light on this issue is: Do you feel like you decided to follow Christ based more on the benefits or consequences that this decision would have on your life now or based more on the benefits or consequences that this decision would have on your life after death? One hundred three persons responded to this question. Fifty-four percent of them said they decided to follow Christ based more on the benefits or consequences that this decision would have on their life now. Twenty-five percent answered that they made this decision more with life after death in mind, and 13 percent indicated that both life-now and life-after-death factors influenced their decision (8 percent responded in ways that could not be clearly evaluated for inclusion in one of the three prior categories). If we allow the 13 percent who responded with "both" to be included in each of the other two categories, we see that 67 percent of the respondents experienced this-life influences in their Christ-following decision while 38 percent were motivated by next-life influences. This equals a ratio of 1.76 to 1.

A final question that merits consideration in this section is: Imagine that you are talking with a non-Christian friend about Jesus, and your friend has arrived at a point of interest concerning the Christian life. If your friend asks you, why should I become a Christian? how would you respond? Ninety-eight persons responded to this question, giving a total of 247 responses that may be grouped into sixteen categories. The results are portrayed in Table 4.3. As the table indicates, only 7 percent of the responses made direct reference to eternal life ("eternal life," "life after death," "live forever with God," and so on). We might choose to broaden this category by including "forgiveness," for some respondents who mentioned forgiveness may have had in mind the heavenly benefit that forgiveness implies. We could also consider including "freedom" for the same reason, though this might be a bit more of a stretch. Even if we include these categories, this would only raise the percentage of next-life references to thirteen, which means that 87 percent of the responses pertain to life here and now. This represents a ratio of 6.7 to 1.

To stretch the point even more, let us assume that the "emotional well-being" category implies a relationship to the next life. For example, a person may experience peace in this life because they feel that things are "settled" concerning the next life. Even if we include this category (the largest single category) in the next-life responses, only 30 percent of the total responses would be related to the next life, while 70 percent would be related to this life. This represents a ratio of 2.3 to 1.

Table 4.3. Responses to Being Asked Why I Should Become a Christian (N=247)

Category	n	%
Emotional well-being	42	17
Change/improve your life	36	15
Other	28	11
Purpose, meaning, fulfillment	22	9
Eternal life	18	7
Relationship with God	15	6
Changed my life, my story	14	6
Guidance/wisdom	13	5
Why not?	11	4
Love/acceptance	10	4
Forgiveness	8	3
Freedom	8	3
Depends on person (contextualize)	7	3
Invite to church, check it out	6	2
Never alone	5	2
Christian community	4	2

The comprehensive results of these four questions are portrayed in Table 4.4. We discover that the average ratio of this-life references to next-life references among these four questions is 4.2 to 1. In relation to these four questions, over four times as many respondents leaned toward this-life answers as toward next-life answers.

Table 4.4. Comparison of This-Life References to Next-Life References

Question	This-Life (%)	Next-Life (%)	Ratio
What does "life in Christ" mean?	90	10	9 to 1
What is "good" about "the good news"?	78	22	3.8 to 1
Christ-following decision based on this-life or next-life benefits/consequences?	67	38[1]	1.8 to 1
Why become a Christian?	70	30	2.3 to 1
Average ratio of all four questions			4.2 to 1

Relational versus Individual Dynamics in the Journey of Following Jesus

Another recurring theme in this project is how relational interactions fit into the journey of following Jesus. Christian living is intended to include relationships with God, others persons, and all of God's creation. The role of relating to God's creation had not yet strongly surfaced in the early stages of my project when I designed the interview questions, so there is no significant data regarding that dimension of Christ-following. However, there is significant data regarding the role of relating with God and other human beings.

The first question to deal with here is: Would you characterize Christ-following as a private affair between an individual person and Jesus, a social affair that includes other people, or something else? Of the 114 respondents, 73 percent said both, 11 percent said private, and 16 percent said social. Combining the both responses and the social responses, we learn that 89 percent of the interviewees believe that Christ-following involves other people. This constitutes a ratio of 8.1 to 1.

Another question pertinent to this theme is: Who or what was influential in your initial decision to follow Christ? Table 4.5 illustrates the breakdown of the 150 responses. If we exclude the God category and the Other category, we discern that 80 percent of the responses indicate that another person was influential in the respondents' initial decision to follow Christ. The responses to these questions clearly demonstrate that the interviewees place a high value on the role of relationships with other people in their journey toward making a Christ-following decision, as well as in their consequent Christ-following life.[2]

Table 4.5. Responses to Influences in Your Initial Decision to Follow Christ (N=150)

Category	n	%
Parent	33	22
Pastor/youth leader/Sunday school teacher	33	22
Other	25	17
Other family	21	14
Christian community	13	9
Friend	11	7
Spouse	10	7
God	4	3

The Importance of Emotional Well-Being among Recent Converts

In chapter 3, I suggested that we should strive for an organic synthesis between relating with God and receiving God's other tangible blessings. What, therefore, are some categories of responses concerning God's other tangible blessings that are prevalent among recent converts?[3] I analyzed

2. One caveat I would make is that I am curious as to how the phrasing of the second question influenced the responses. I designed the question to ask both *who* and/or *what* was influential in the initial Christ-following decision, but I began with the who. I wonder if the responses might have been any different had I reversed the order of the who and the what. I believe the people-related answers to the question as I phrased it were so prevalent that the essential point concerning the involvement of relationships in the Christ-following journey still holds, but perhaps the percentages would have been different.

3. I am especially interested in the perspective of recent converts because one of the important dimensions of evangelism is the need to attend to questions and issues that

four questions to identify which categories of responses ranked highest among recent converts. Taking the top two response categories from each question, the results are displayed in Table 4.6. The table indicates that the category of emotional well-being seems to be an important one for recent converts in regard to these four questions. It is the leading category for two of the four questions and was tied for third with another one. It also seems like a natural fit to think about emotional well-being along with the response category of love, which leads the way in relation to the question regarding the essential gospel message.

Table 4.6. Top Two Categories of Responses from Recent Converts

Question	Highest Response Rate from Recent Converts	Second-Highest Response Rate from Recent Converts
Why become a Christian?	Emotional well-being (42%)	Improve or change your life (32%)
Good dimensions of Good news	Bible (or the four Gospels) (29%)	Guidance for living (16%)
Life in Christ	Emotional well-being (58%)	Fullness or abundance (35%)
Essential gospel message	Love (45%)	Believe or accept Jesus (19%)

The Life God Intends Is to Impact Every Dimension of Our Lives

Another theme that arose previously is that the life God intends for us in Christ is to impact every dimension of our lives. To help us investigate this theme from the perspective of the interviews, we now turn to the question: What difference has Jesus made in your life? Sixty-seven persons were

non-Christians are actually addressing, rather than those which Christians *think* they are (or *should* be) addressing. It is this notion that prompts Donald McGavran (*Understanding Church Growth*, 54–66, 192) to advocate field research to help Christians discover what *actually* helps persons choose to become Christ-followers, rather than falling back on practices that we *think will* work or *ought* to work because they worked for us or because we like them. He refers to *effective* evangelism. He also suggests that "recent converts are a rich source of insight" (*Understanding Church Growth*, 11).

asked this question, with a total of 140 responses given.[4] Of those 140 responses, the leading category was emotional well-being, with forty-two responses, equaling 30 percent. The second largest category was one that I titled everything/new/changed, with twenty-two responses, constituting 16 percent. These responses included such comments as "everything changed," "He made all the difference," and "I'm a new person." The third category, having to do with guidance, wisdom, and/or a new perspective, had eighteen responses, constituting 13 percent. Three additional categories were tied at 9 percent. They were (a) made me more loving, caring, and/or generous; (b) meaning/purpose/fulfillment; and (c) Jesus helped me trust God's plan, provision, and/or protection.

It was obvious as I listened to these responses that many interviewees had experienced pervasive changes in their lives as a result of following Jesus. One person said: "180-degree turnaround; my mindset, how I view life, how I approach life; being real versus unreal; having true peace and joy and love versus faking it; it's just tremendous; I would not be where I am today without him for sure."[5] Another respondent spoke of "demonstrative changes in my life: I'm more patient, more tolerant, more compassionate, and many people notice this. My wife says 'I got a new husband.'"[6] Another person said: "Jesus has saved my marriage, he healed my son from Tourette's, he has helped me forgive my father for his sexual abuse . . . he gives me direction all day long, and shields me with his armor."[7] Another recent convert declared that "I feel whole, I am complete now . . . My family sees a very different person now . . . they are trying to get used to the new 'Jane.' He has turned my life completely around."[8] Another interviewee said that "he's changed everything and what he hasn't changed he still needs to."[9]

Not all respondents gave answers that were so pervasive, as indicated by the fact that only twenty-two of the 140 responses fell into the everything/new/changed category, but the spirit of pervasiveness was present in

4. Note that most questions were asked of more than sixty-seven persons. This question was asked of fewer persons than the other questions because it was added to the list of questions after interviews had been completed with the first two churches.

5. Interview with author, Effingham, IL, July 14, 2010. All interviews were confidential; the names of interviewees are withheld by mutual agreement.

6. Interview with author, Mt. Pleasant, SC, June 10, 2010.

7. Ibid., June 9, 2010.

8. Interview with author, McDonough, GA, May 11, 2010.

9. Interview with author, Effingham, IL, July 13, 2010.

many of the interviewees, even though they did not all use that type of terminology. From this perspective, one might possibly say that many of the respondents believe that the life in Christ they are experiencing has indeed touched all spheres or dimensions of their lives. But is that really true? Remember the distinction I made in chapter 6 concerning this point. I observed that some Christians understand that the Christ-following life is intended to be relational and therefore should not be overly privatized. However, the impact of following Christ still remains limited to them and a small portion of their relational network. Jesus has given them a whole new outlook, an entirely different way of viewing and experiencing their daily existence, but that change has not impacted them at the deep worldview level. Is any light shed on this issue from the interview responses?

Due to the nature of my primary research interests, the kinds of questions that might have elicited more enlightening information concerning these issues were not included. This would be a very interesting topic for future research. Nevertheless, perhaps we can glean some tentative insight from the questions that were asked. My first comment would be to note that 9 percent of the responses to the question, what difference has Jesus made in your life? specifically referred to Jesus helping the interviewees become more loving and caring of others, more generous to help people in various circumstances. This is not a huge percentage by any means, but it does illustrate that some of the respondents were aware of this change that following Christ had made in their lives, and were aware of it strongly enough to be able to name it. We see a similar dynamic in the answers to the question regarding what life in Christ means. Six percent of the responses to that question involved loving or serving others, and 5 percent referred to being Christ-like (using descriptors such as *selfless, kind, good, patient,* and *humble*). In the question about the essential Christian message, fourteen of the 162 responses referred to loving others, which constitutes 9 percent. In response to the question regarding what Jesus meant by abundant life in John 10:10, 11 percent (twenty-seven of 251) of the responses fell into the serving, related to others category. Viewing these questions as a whole, we see that 9 to 10 percent of the responses were linked in some way to a focus on helping, loving, or serving others. It is impossible to tell whether this focus on others had made its way outside the smaller relational networks of the respondents to impact their views and actions concerning larger issues.

Moreover, this means that approximately 90 percent of the responses did not mention any focus on others. This tentatively suggests that most respondents had not reached a point in their Christ-following journey where the pervasive changes they felt they had experienced (and were continuing to experience) had impacted them at a deep worldview level to the point that it influenced their thoughts or actions regarding larger issues of politics, economics, justice, creation care, and so on. A question that bears contemplation is whether this issue of all dimensions of our lives being involved in the life that God intends for us should be addressed in the ministry of discipleship, the ministry of evangelism, or some combination of both. I lean toward suggesting that it should be at least tentatively addressed in evangelism, and then more fully addressed in discipleship. This, however, poses a dilemma. If we attempt to highlight all the issues that are important in the Christ-following journey within the ministry of evangelism, how do we distinguish between evangelism and discipleship? Moreover, if we include all the important issues in evangelism, then might we run the risk of overwhelming the non-Christian with a message that is far too complex and will appear to be overly burdensome, rather than liberating and life-giving? I will address this further in the next chapter.

Joy, Delight, or Happiness

An additional theme I wish to address is that of the joy, delight, or happiness that God intends for us in following Jesus. Using six interview questions as the basis for my analysis, I examined the interview notes to identify how many individual respondents (as distinct from responses) referred to joy, happiness, laughter, or excitement.[10] The results are displayed in Table 4.7. Using the Total column as our first indicator, we see that the cumulative total of respondents for the six questions is 592. There were ninety-seven specific references made to joy, happiness, excitement, or laughter among

---

10. The six questions are (1) In the Gospel of John, there are a lot of verses about life. In your experience and understanding, what does "life in Christ" mean? (2) Imagine that you are talking with a non-Christian friend about Jesus, and your friend has arrived at a point of interest concerning the Christian life. If your friend asks you why should I become a Christian? how would you respond? (3) Sometimes we refer to the "gospel" as "the good news." In your experience and/or understanding, what are some of the "good" dimensions of "the good news"? (4) Is there any sense in which you are more alive now than before you became a Christ-follower? (5) What do you think Jesus means in John 10:10 when he says, "I came that they may have life and have it abundantly"? (6) What difference has Jesus made in your life?

the 592 respondents.[11] This represents 16 percent. We may safely say, therefore, that roughly one in six persons include some form of joy, delight, or happiness in how they conceptualize or experience the Christ-following life. This suggests that this theme may warrant at least modest consideration in evangelistic theory and practice.

Table 4.7. Responses among Participants Regarding the Mention of Joy, Delight, Happiness, or Excitement

Question	Total		
	N	n	%
More alive now?	125	26	21
Abundant life	98	25	26
What difference Jesus made	67	11	16
Life in Christ	111	24	22
Good re. the Good News	93	3	3
Why become a Christian?	98	8	8
Cumulative totals	592	97	16

Consistency of Christians Regarding Their Own Experience versus Their Evangelism Participation

I would now like to shift to an analysis of research questions taken as pairs, in order to evaluate how consistent the evangelistically gifted leaders, recent converts, and staff are concerning their own experiences of the Christ-following life versus how they embody and communicate the Christ-following life with non-believers.[12] I wish to query, for example, whether it might

11. This is obvious, but to avoid misunderstanding please allow me to remind you that there are not 592 separate individuals represented here, because the same people responded to all six questions.

12. Because most KILs (key influential leaders) were interviewed in small group settings, the interview notes do not lend themselves well to this type of comparison. One can discern from the notes how many KILs offered comments and what the comments were, but one cannot discern which individual person made which comment, which makes comparison of paired answers impossible.

be possible that some people initially chose to follow Christ based on the benefits or consequences related to this life, but as they have experienced more time in the Christ-following journey, they have begun to more fully emphasize the benefits or consequences of Christ-following related to life after death. Furthermore, has that growing emphasis influenced them to relate with non-Christians primarily in terms of next-life benefits or consequences as opposed to this-life benefits or consequences? Conversely, might some Christians have chosen to follow Christ based on next-life issues, but they have experienced such a positive transformation in this life that their predominant relationship with non-believers focuses on this life? To begin this exploration, I reviewed the evangelistically gifted leader, recent convert, and staff responses to the following pair of questions: Do you feel like you decided to follow Christ based more on the benefits or consequences that this decision would have on your life now or based more on the benefits or consequences that this decision would have on your life after death? and How would you respond if your non-Christian friend asked you why they should become a Christian? Thirty-two (82 percent) of the evangelistically gifted leaders gave consistent responses to these two questions, while seven (18 percent) gave inconsistent responses. The overall percentage among staff responses was almost identical. Twenty-one (81 percent) of the staff interviewees gave consistent responses and five (19 percent) offered inconsistent ones. Regarding the recent converts, twenty-seven (87 percent) of the recent convert responses were consistent and four (13 percent) were inconsistent, making this group the most consistent of the three.

I now want to compare the responses to the question, why should I become a Christian? with those given to a second question to gauge the level of consistency between the responses. Results for the question, why should I become a Christian? are portrayed in Table 4.8.

Table 4.8. Responses to Reasons for Becoming a Christian (N=247)

Category	N	%
Emotional well-being	42	17
Change/improve your life	36	15
Other[2]	28	11
Purpose, meaning, fulfillment	22	9
Eternal life	18	7
Relationship with God	15	6
Changed my life, my story	14	6
Guidance/wisdom	13	5
Why not?	11	4
Love/acceptance	10	4
Forgiveness	8	3
Freedom	8	3
Depends on person (contextualize)	7	3
Invite to church, check it out	6	2
Never alone	5	2
Christian community	4	2

The question I wish to compare this with is the following: What do you believe are some of the things your non-Christian friends think about the most? One hundred eight people responded to this question, giving 240 total responses. The results are found in Table 4.9. The first thing to point out is that money and finances is the leading category for the second question, but does not appear at all as a response category to the first question.[13] Thirty-seven of the 240 responses refer to finances, which constitutes 15 percent. If we add in the two categories of material stuff and job/careers, this number increases to seventy-four of 240, for a percentage of 31. In other words, almost one in three of the responses to this category

13. For the first question, a minimum of four similar responses was required to merit a separate response category. Two of the ninety-eight respondents (2 percent) suggested that provision was one of the reasons a non-Christian friend should become a Christian. These two responses are represented in the Other category.

refers to something related to finances, and yet this category is completely absent from the response categories pertaining to the first question. I do not suggest that it should necessarily appear among those responses, for it would be theologically inappropriate to suggest to a non-Christian that they should become a Christian so their money problems would be solved; at least this is probably how most Christians would respond if asked that specific question. However, please allow me to play devil's advocate for a moment. If following Jesus helps us set new priorities in our lives that are more fully aligned with God's intentions, and if those new priorities include how we spend our money, is it not possible that many of our money problems would be solved as we lived according to those God-guided priorities? I have tried to make the case in this project that abundant financial provision (not necessarily prosperity) is included as one of the dimensions of the full life in Jesus that God intends for us. If this is the case, why should we not include financial health as one of the reasons a person should become a Christian, especially if that is an issue that many non-Christians think about? Yet, financial health was not mentioned often enough (a minimum of four times) to be classified as a response category for this question.

Table 4.9. Responses Concerning What Non-Christian Friends Think about the Most (N=240)

Category	n	%
Money/finances	37	15
Other[3]	29	12
Material stuff	19	8
Drugs/alcohol/sex	19	8
Job/careers	18	8
Themselves	18	8
Reputation, self-image, acceptance, status	16	7
Christian-related[4]	16	7
Short-term present	10	4
Children	9	4
Family	8	3

Fulfillment/happiness/satisfaction	8	3
Success/power/influence	7	3
Pleasure/partying/entertainment	7	3
Big life questions (meaning, purpose, identity, significance)	6	3
Other relationships	5	2
Fears/worry	5	2
Marriage	3	1

Important Considerations for Evangelistic Theory and Practice

The exploration of notes from conversations with Christ-followers in local congregations highlights five important areas for consideration in evangelistic theory and practice:

- In whatever way we may choose to include the possibility of new life in Christ in our evangelistic vision and ministry, we must include references to experiencing positive benefits in this life, if we want to resonate well with non-believers.[14]

- The research data prompts us to consider an emphasis on the fact that Christians should be made aware of the profound influence they may have on people in their relational networks. This knowledge could increase individual motivation for evangelism, and it could also motivate congregational leaders to provide more opportunities for equipping congregational participants for the ministry of evangelism in their relational networks.

- The strong prevalence of emotional well-being among responses from recent converts encourages us to deem emotional relevance as an important dimension of the Christ-following experience, to

---

14. In addition to resonating well with non-Christians, an inclusion of this-life impact in following Christ honors the holistic perspective of Christ-following that is seen in the Bible. We do not simply follow Jesus to gain entrance to heaven. We also follow him to serve as instruments of his life-giving purposes for other persons and for creation.

the extent that it should be included in ministries that will involve non-Christians.[15]

- Financial health can serve as a solid connection point for relationship with some non-Christians. Therefore, the evangelistic community should struggle more fully with how to address this topic in a way that is theologically appropriate, honors the abundant provision that is biblically and theologically sound, yet does not bleed over into an inappropriate focus on an unbiblical prosperity gospel.

- Individual Christians and congregations should be encouraged to include the dimension of joy and happiness in their evangelistic visions and ministries, for this would strike a deep chord within some non-believers. This was not a major theme, but it was a sufficiently strong theme to indicate that some persons would be encouraged toward Christ by witnessing and hearing of the joyful delight that is a dimension of following him.

I will now move to the final chapter, in which I will tie together what we have learned from the field research, the selected material regarding the Old Testament and John's Gospel, and the exploration into insights from selected theologians. I will then point out some of the beginning contours of an evangelistic vision that is based on the biblical theme of life.

15. George Hunter (*Apostolic Congregation*, 31) has attempted to awaken Christians to the prime importance of "emotional relevance" in reaching non-Christians. He believes that (at least in the West) we have been misled by the Enlightenment view that people are primarily rational beings. Conversely, Hunter proposes that "human beings are essentially *emotional* creatures who are sometimes capable of thinking!" Leaders of effective churches, therefore, know that choosing to follow Christ is a journey that involves our emotional well-being. Thus, "effective churches begin with people where they are; they consider people's emotional agendas and their struggle for emotional freedom."

8

The Beginning Contours of a Life-Based Evangelistic Vision

The Question that Started It All, and Where It Has Taken Us

THE GENESIS OF THIS project was a simple yet vital question: What are the implications for evangelism if one places a strong emphasis on the biblical theme of life? This question led to the premise that the biblical theme of life may be viewed as one of the primary themes of the Bible and, as such, provides a strong and helpful foundation for the theory and practice of evangelism.

In the first two chapters, I gave support for this premise and discussed a range of related issues. One of these issues is that the concept of eternal life refers not only to chronological eternity but also to the quality of the life of the age-to-come in our current experience of full life in Jesus. Therefore evangelism should not be limited only to helping persons prepare for entry into heaven, but should also fully address how to communicate God's intentions that all people experience a full life in Jesus prior to physical death on earth, and invite people into that full life.

A second issue is the question of how to relate the kingdom of God motif in the Synoptic Gospels with the consequent proposal that an experience of full life was God's original intention for us in creation, and therefore, is also God's current goal for our life in Jesus Christ. Additional vital concepts, such as promise, covenant, and redemption, may be viewed as instruments or means to reach that goal. The concept of kingdom is a bit more difficult to conceive of as instrument or means, for it portrays more of a sense of the realm in which God's full life is experienced rather than one of the instruments that contributes to that full life. Kingdom, therefore, should perhaps be considered more as a parallel concept that provides a different symbolic reference for understanding God's purposes for us. *Life* refers to God's ultimate intentions for us, and *kingdom* refers to the fact that God is the creator and ruler of the systemic entity or arena in which life is generated and experienced. However, even if we acknowledge kingdom as a parallel concept, we must also recognize that the theme of life is biblically and theologically prior, and thus helps ground evangelism in God's creation (both God's original creation and God's new creation in Christ). This creation emphasis is much more faithful to God's original intention for humanity and all of creation than is the emphasis some evangelistic visions place on humanity's fall.

Howard Snyder observes how John Wesley's focus on creation as the starting place for Christian theology helps ground theology and evangelism in the positive dimensions of persons being created in the image of God, rather than in the negative dimensions of sin and the fall. Wesley does not ignore sin, but neither does he choose sin as the starting place. Snyder writes, "The Wesleyan lens starts with good news: A good God created good people in an ecologically balanced creation that God pronounced 'very good.' In the Wesleyan telling, the gospel story moves from the good news of creation in God's image, to the bad news of sin and distortion, to the even better news of redemption and new creation through Jesus Christ by the power of the Spirit."[1] This is the essential point I am making in relation to creation as the starting point for an evangelistic vision grounded in the biblical theme of life. We begin with God's good and positive intentions. This provides a more appropriate biblical and theological foundation for theology and evangelism.

In chapters 3 and 4, I made a brief exploration into the field of biblical studies, focusing on the theme of life in the Old Testament and the gospel of John.

The Old Testament material revealed a strong emphasis on God as the living God who invites us into an experience of full life through relationship with and obedience to God. This experience of full life also involves relationships with other people in community, not only as an intangible (or "spiritual") experience, but also as a very tangible one. Life as God intends was envisioned in the Old Testament in terms of bountiful harvests,

---

1. Snyder, *Yes in Christ*, 20.

reproductive fertility, physical health, delight, security in the land, victory over enemies, and a long life.

In exilic and post-exilic times, the focus leaned far more heavily toward conceiving of life as relationship with God, with a postponement of tangible blessings to some future time. The priestly tradition attempted an organic synthesis of God's tangible blessings with the supreme blessing of knowing God, but this synthesis was seldom successful. Two tensions or continuums emerged. One was this tension or continuum between conceiving of life in terms of God's tangible blessings versus the blessing of knowing God. The other was a tension or continuum that involved the experience of God's full-life intentions for us now versus some future time.

The investigation of John's theology of life revealed the same two dynamics. Regarding the life-now versus life-then dynamic, there is a modest consensus among scholars that John's Gospel includes more of a life-now emphasis than do the Synoptic Gospels. Regarding the "knowing God" versus "God's other tangible gifts" dynamic, a great deal of stress is placed on knowing God. This is best expressed as believing in, knowing, obeying, and abiding in, Jesus. At the same time, however, John vividly portrays persons being healed, fed, and forgiven by Jesus. Therefore, though we should not downplay the vital importance of knowing God as the central experience of the life that Jesus came to bring, neither should we downplay the other tangible gifts that Jesus grants to his followers, such as health, provision, joy, peace, purpose, human relationships, and much more. To use the sheep and shepherding imagery of John 10, the sheep indeed must know the shepherd's voice, but they are also daily led by the shepherd from the sheepfold out into abundant pasture.

The presence of both human and divine involvement in the experience of full life is an additional continuum that emerges from John's Gospel. John portrays a strong element of both. It is clear that God initiates the possibility of full life in Jesus and extends the invitation to us, but it is also clear that human beings play a role not only in accepting that invitation but also in the communication and extension of it. In terms of evangelism, this suggests that evangelism begins with God, but God also intends, invites, and desires that God's people be active participants in the evangelization process. A final continuum or tension that is raised in John's Gospel is one between the individual and communal (or relational) dimensions of the full life that is involved in the Christ-following journey. There is no question that John wishes to emphasize that individuals are called and invited to believe, know, obey, and abide in Jesus, and in so doing receive full life. At the same time, however, John strongly emphasizes the unity of believers and Jesus's insistence that they love one another.

The investigation of John's theology of life also helped reveal the inter-related nature of the incarnation and the cross in John's Gospel. Combining the differing perspectives of Gail R. O'Day and Craig Koester, one can see that John's Gospel presents a portrayal of the pre-incarnational Jesus who was God (and was with God); the incarnational Jesus who came to earth in fullness to help us know him; the wise and powerful Jesus who taught, healed, raised, and fed; the compassionate Jesus who died to demonstrate the depth of God's love; and the resurrected and exalted Jesus who gives us the Holy Spirit to guide us in how to continue abiding in him (Jesus), and in so doing experience full and vital life. This inclusion of the varying dimensions of Jesus's life provides a solid theological and biblical founda-tion for life-based evangelism. We are invited to a full life in Jesus, and that full life is directly linked to the fullness of who Jesus is and was, as well as what he experienced in our stead and on our behalf. This implies that the ministry of evangelism must be envisioned comprehensively. I will explore this theme more fully at a later point in this chapter.

Chapters 5 and 6 described an investigation of the work of selected theologians concerning the life theme and related issues. From this investi-gation, eight themes emerged as consistently important:

- Our experience of life must remain tied to our relationship with and commitment to God who is the source and giver of life.

- Life as God intends is relational and communal.

- God intends that the life God gives through Jesus and the Spirit will impact all spheres and dimensions of life (such as personal, familial, communal, relational, social, economic, political, and cultural).

- God desires holistic flourishing for us.

- The life of holistic flourishing God intends will include a biblically ap-propriate understanding and experience of joy, delight, or happiness.

- Life is God's ultimate goal for God's creation and God's creatures.

- There is a balance or tension between life-now and life-then.

- Life as God intends cannot be divorced from God's created material world.

In chapter 7, I engaged in an analysis of the field research data that I collected from interviews with 153 persons in eight congregations. Based on this analysis, I discerned five important areas for consideration in evangelistic theory and practice. First is the need for evangelistic vision and ministry to include the possibility of experiencing positive benefits in this life if we want to resonate well with non-believers. Second, Christians should be made aware of the profound influence they may have on people in their relational networks. Third, emotional relevance is an important dimension of the Christ-following experience, and should therefore be included in ministries that will involve non-Christians. Fourth, the evangelistic community should struggle more fully with how to address the theme of financial health in a way that is theologically appropriate, honors the abundant provision that is biblically and theologically sound, yet does not bleed over into an inappropriate focus on an unbiblical prosperity gospel. Fifth, individual Christians and congregations should be encouraged to include the dimension of joy and happiness in their evangelistic visions and ministries.

Original Research Questions: The Four Clusters

This brief summary of insights that surfaced during this research project illustrates the diverse nature of a life-based evangelistic vision. To avoid undue redundancy, each insight or issue will not be revisited. However, it would be helpful to return to the original four clusters of research question claims that were presented in the first chapter, and to discuss how the insights and issues that have emerged during this project relate to those questions. This will assist in highlighting the most important implications of life-based evangelism. The first cluster relates to the gospel. The second has to do with the biblical theme of life (focusing on insights from biblical studies). The third involves the relationship between the biblical theme of life, the kingdom of God, and eternal life. The fourth entails the relational dimensions of full life in Christ.

What, therefore, has this research project revealed regarding these clusters of questions? In responding to this query we will begin with the second cluster (the biblical theme of life), because it lays the foundation for the other three.

The Biblical Theme of Life

Life as originally intended by God in creation, and as now intended by God in Jesus Christ, is envisioned as a full, vibrant, joyous experience of living in relationship with God (in Christ), with other people, and with all of creation. Our experience of full life must be rooted in our acknowledgement of and relationship with God as Creator and Sovereign, and any attempt to experience life outside that acknowledgement and relationship will fall far short of God's intentions for us.

As we live out our commitment to and relationship with God, we also relate with other people and with God's creation, offering mutual support and sharing. This lays the groundwork for a life of holistic flourishing that we experience spiritually, relationally, physically, environmentally, emotionally, provisionally (finances, basic needs, and so on), socially, and politically. The life God intends and envisions is to impact every sphere of our existence, so that nothing in our life is left untouched by the God whom we worship, serve, and relate with.

A particular emphasis in the Old Testament is that life in God involves the material world, so that there is no false dichotomy construed between what is material and what is spiritual. Bountiful harvests, reproductive fertility, security in the land, physical health, life long-lived, and success in all endeavors: these are dimensions of the good life that the Hebrew people envisioned as they worshipped, served, and obeyed God.

As we move into the Gospel of John we learn that this life is only made possible through Jesus, and Jesus must be understood at this point holistically. Life is made possible through his incarnation, birth, life, death, resurrection, and exaltation.[2] We must not, for example, attempt to "go around" the cross but through it. Likewise, we must "go through" the incarnation, understanding that not only in Jesus's death do we experience life, but we also experience life because He Who is God became Life for us on earth. Thus, we do not avoid the cross, but neither do we emphasize the cross to the point that we eliminate the vital importance of everything else that surrounds the Jesus "event."

It is not sufficient, for example, to say that we have appropriated the benefits of atonement for our salvation or forgiveness if we neglect the teachings of Jesus to be agents of peace, justice, and love. Conversely, we

2. In like manner, Thomas Oden (*Word of Life*, 11) refers to the gospel as "the good news of God's own coming, the cumulative event of the sending, coming, living, dying, and continuing life of this incomparable One."

will not experience the full life that God intends if we focus on being agents of peace, justice, and love without an accompanying emphasis on Jesus's death and resurrection and the role they play in our forgiveness and healing (salvation, restoration, and rescue). Full life comes, therefore, when we trust in (completely give ourselves to) Jesus and follow him, obeying his commands and guidelines for how to live. Additionally, we are intended to experience a strong measure of full, vibrant life here on earth before we die, and we will experience an even fuller, more final measure of that life in God's presence after death. This current "strong measure" of full life will include provision, purpose, joy, peace, justice, worship, service, and much more. It is envisioned as a restoration of the original experience of full, vibrant life that God intended in creation.

To crystalize what this project has revealed concerning the biblical theme of life:

> Life as God intends us to experience it in Jesus is a holistic, relational flourishing of people, relational networks, communities, and God's creation. It is rooted in a full-bodied trust in and following of Jesus (this includes knowing, obeying, and abiding in him), which brings us forgiveness and initiates a life of wholeness (redemption) and reconciliation (with God, ourselves, and others). This life is characterized by peace, justice, love, purpose, and provision in all dimensions of existence.

An Initial Life-Based Description of the Gospel

How does a strong focus on the biblical theme of life inform our understanding and communication of the gospel? What is the good news that we embody and share with non-Christians? What are we inviting them to embrace, or take up, or do? Based on what we have learned about the biblical theme of life, the good news may be viewed as follows:

> Through a full-bodied trust in and following of Jesus, we receive forgiveness and are initiated into a life of wholeness (redemption) and reconciliation. This life is best described as a holistic and relational flourishing of people, relational networks, communities, and God's creation; and this flourishing will be characterized by joy, peace, justice, love, purpose, and provision, in all dimensions of life.

This description of the gospel is based on the description of life that was delineated in the previous section, most of which was based on the insights gained from the research in biblical studies and theology. However, these insights regarding the gospel may be deepened by referring back to the insights that emerged in the analysis of field research data.

Deepening the Initial Life-Based Gospel Understanding: Emotional Well-Being

Notice that joy, peace, and love are included in the aforementioned life-based gospel description. We recall that in embodying and communicating the good news with non-Christians, the field research indicates that we should be aware of the importance of emotional well-being. This suggests that emotional well-being should be a dimension of the gospel we are consistently exemplifying and are ready to verbally share whenever the Holy Spirit leads us in that direction. To maintain consistency in our evangelism, we would also therefore want to envision how to extend an invitation to follow Jesus that is based on emotional well-being. For example, one might say: "I have found in my life that I discover more consistent joy when I follow Jesus's leadership in my life and try to be the person and partner he designed me to be. Would you like to experience more consistent joy as well? Then I invite you to choose today to follow him and partner with him in his life-giving mission in the world." Or one might say, "I've had a lot more peace over the past several months, and it seems to go back to a decision I made to trust God with respect to my children. I still fret about them occasionally, but whenever I remind myself that I have chosen to entrust them to God's care, a deep peace settles over me. Perhaps you would like to try trusting God's care for your children as well, and see if you might gain a greater level of peace." These are just two examples of ways one might make a verbal connection between emotional well-being and an invitation to begin a life of following Jesus.

Moreover, the awareness of emotional relevance should not be limited to individual opportunities to invite persons to follow Christ, but should also be an integral part of congregational ministries in general. A life-based evangelism ministry, for example, could urge congregations to create environments of love and acceptance in the communal spaces where the congregation most often gathers. It could help foster relational groupings that provide a sense of security and belonging. It could strive to influence the worship leadership team to include moments of joy and celebration in the worship services. It could encourage pastors to preach sermon series on emotional issues and link the biblical truths concerning those issues to the full life that God intends for us. These are just a few examples of ways that a life-based evangelism ministry could promote emotional relevance in a congregation's overall ministry.

Deepening the Initial Life-Based Gospel Understanding: Financial Health

A second broadening of the life-based gospel conceptualization that the field research suggests relates to financial health.[3] One in three of the interviewees believed that their non-Christian friends think or worry about financial health. As stated previously, I don't suggest that limitless prosperity be considered part of the good news concerning full life in Christ, but abundant provision is an appropriate image to include in the message we embody and share. It would be entirely fitting, for example, for a Christ-follower to say to a non-believing friend: "Yes, I understand. I used to worry a lot about money too, and I still do every once in a while. But about two years ago I discovered that when I follow Jesus's priorities for how to manage the resources he provides me with, my financial health improved dramatically. I truly cannot explain it, because I make the same salary today as then, but somehow following Jesus's guidelines for finances has made a difference. Would you like to try following his financial guidelines for a few months and see what happens?" Obviously, the invitation being extended here is not to repent, ask for forgiveness, accept Jesus as Lord and Savior, receive Jesus in your heart, or any of the other standard invitations that we are accustomed to. In the context of the financial health dimension of the gospel, however, it is a perfectly appropriate invitation to get someone started on the road toward following Jesus.

Moreover, the willingness to extend this kind of invitation honors the fact that just as following Christ is a lifelong journey, so too is the decision to follow Christ experienced by many people as a process, a series of varying decisions that eventually leads to a more specifically cognizant decision to follow Jesus.

---

3. This is why *provision* is included in the aforementioned life-based gospel description.

Offer Them Life

Deepening the Initial Life-Based Gospel Understanding:
Being Loosed from One Mental Script

An additional insight from the field research that impacts a life-based gospel understanding is that some Christians continue to be bound by the "old and standard" mental script that includes references to images such as salvation, forgiveness, repentance, ABCs, and the sinner's prayer. This helps us at two points. First, it reminds us that developing an evangelistic vision based on the biblical theme of life provides us with different images we can access in the ministry of evangelism. For example, we could invite persons to "live life as God intends" rather than "accept Christ as your Lord and Savior," or we could encourage people to "partner with Jesus in bringing full life to others" instead of asking them to "use your spiritual gifts to build up the church and minister to the world," or we could suggest that "Jesus came into the world to bring full life" rather than "Jesus came into the world to save sinners." A life-based understanding of evangelism adds to the options available to us in our inventory of images.

The second point to emphasize here comes from the opposite perspective. Just as we do not want to be limited to one primary mental script, we also want to avoid suggesting that life-based images become the new script that binds us. We can make a strong case for considering the life theme as a primary theme of the Bible, but the intent is not to discard all other evangelistic visions and replace them with a life-based vision. Instead the goal is to argue strongly and cogently enough for the life theme so that it would be allowed its place among other evangelistic portrayals and add to the evangelistic possibilities available to us. The gospel is multifaceted. People and cultural contexts are multifaceted too. Therefore, we will be much better served by an expansion of evangelistic theology, imagery, and language, as opposed to a simple discarding of the old for replacement with the new. In certain contexts with certain people, it is appropriate to speak primarily of Jesus as Lord and Savior who forgives our sins and calls us to a life of discipleship and ministry. In other contexts, with other people, it is more helpful to speak primarily of the possibility of experiencing full life on earth as God originally intended, and invite persons to begin that journey.

The Relationship between Life, the Kingdom of God, and Eternal Life

This topic has been addressed at various points throughout this project, so these comments will be brief. In terms of implications for evangelistic theory and practice, two perspectives in particular are pertinent. The first is that *life* expresses God's intention for God's creation, while the *kingdom of God* may be viewed as a parallel concept that expresses the arena in which life is experienced. Even though kingdom may be viewed as a parallel concept, life remains theologically and biblically prior to kingdom because of its close connection with the creation narratives. With this life-based perspective, therefore, evangelism is more directly grounded in the creation narratives, and this is the best biblical and theological starting place. Embodying and communicating the possibility of full life in Jesus with non-believers and helping them embrace that full life makes sense, therefore, biblically, theologically, and evangelistically.

The second perspective that is especially pertinent is that the use of *eternal* as a descriptor of the life that God makes possible through Jesus involves life-now dimensions as well as life-then dimensions. This has been discussed at length, so three brief remarks will suffice at this point. First, the field research data clearly indicates the benefit of including the possibility of full life now in evangelistic theory and practice. Remember that the ratio of life-now references to life-then references in the research data was four to one. Moreover, the recurrence of life-now references is even more prevalent for recent converts. This data leads us to acknowledge that life-now dimensions of the good news must be given at least equal importance in the ministry of evangelism.

The second point is that the quality of the life that is being offered now is that of the age to come. Jesus has ushered in a caliber of living that is unparalleled. We experience transformation when we follow Jesus and embrace the life he offers. Forgiveness is available. Justice is presupposed. Healing is given. Peace is present. This age-to-come quality of living is evidenced in the biblical narratives, envisioned in the theological material, and observed in the field research. John's vision of Jesus "making all things new" (Revelation 21:6) will come finally and fully to fruition at some future time, but the quality of that newness can be experienced in partial measure even now.

The third remark concerning life-now is that this dimension of the Christ-following journey should not be stressed to the point that the life-then dimension is completely forgotten. Just as we seek an organic synthesis of the blessing of knowing God with the other tangible blessings that God grants in Christ, so too do we seek an organic synthesis of life-now and life-then. We experience an unparalleled caliber of living now due to the age-to-come quality of the life that Jesus brings. However, we also experience an extraordinary caliber of living now because of our faith in the promise of an even fuller experience of God's intentions in the future. With the same breath, therefore, it is appropriate to argue for a stronger life-now dimension in the ministry of evangelism in order to connect well with non-believers, while yet also lobbying for us not to forget the reality of the future vision of the new heaven and the new earth.

The Relational Dimensions of Full Life in Christ

I made an early claim that full life in Christ cannot be experienced, expressed, or shared outside the scope of relationships, nor at the expense of other persons. I solidly substantiated this claim via the biblical studies material, the theology chapter, and the field research data. The ensuing comments, therefore, will be limited to two vital issues: (1) the relational dimension of Christ-following is integral to evangelism and not an add-on, and (2) how this dimension impacts evangelism training.

The Relational Dimension of Full Life in Christ Is Integral to Full Life in Christ

In the U.S. American context, where the independent, individualistic mindset exerts such strong influence, it is important to confirm that the relational dimension of following Christ should not be considered as something that we add on to our understandings at some future point in our Christ-following journey, but rather is essential and integral from the very beginning of that journey. This confirmation is necessary because in spite of the many voices in U.S. American Christianity that have clamored for a fuller integration of the relational and interdependent nature of Christ-following, there is yet a strong tendency to think in privatized, individualistic, isolationist ways. Hiebert notes that this way of thinking is contrary to the Hebraic way of thinking that undergirds the Bible. He writes that "the idea of the . . . autonomous individual is absent in Hebrew thought and biblical teachings," which means that "biblically, relatedness and community are at the heart of the gospel because they are of the essence of God himself."[4] In a similar vein, Lalsangkima Pachuau proposes that it is impossible to even conceive of selfhood apart from relationships, for the self is "a relational being by its very nature," so that "whether identity is conceived as 'given' or as 'constructed', it is a relational entity."[5] Relationality is part and parcel of who the Triune God is, and as persons created in God's image, it is also part and parcel of who we are, or at least of who we are intended to be. This suggests that living in relationship with God, others, and God's creation is an intrinsic dimension of the full life that God intends and makes possible through Jesus. This further suggests that the relational dimension of the Christ-following life must be included in evangelistic ministry.

We hear echoes here of Yoder, Harink, Stone, and others. You may recall, for example, that Stone argues against the type of evangelism that seeks first to convince persons to accept a personal relationship with Christ and then subsequently encourages them to participate in the social and public embodiment of Christ's peaceable reign. He maintains that participation in the social and public embodiment of Christ's peaceable reign through God's people (the church) is part and parcel of conversion, not subsequent to it.[6] It would be helpful to nuance Stone's perspective just a bit. It is true that the relational dimension of the Christ-following life is intrinsic to that life, and not subsequent to it. However, in response to Stone's declaration that the relational dimension of the Christ-following life is offered *as* salvation, it would be more accurate to say that it is offered as an integral *part of* salvation. This confirms that the relational dimension is part of the essential core of the Christ-following life and must not be neglected, but it also confirms that it does not make up the whole of that life. Relationships are crucial and central, but relationships involve individuals, and individuals are invited to make personal decisions regarding the full life that Jesus offers. Given the U.S. American context of this project, it is true that the relational dimensions of the Christ-following journey should be strongly emphasized. However, this emphasis should not be so strong that evangelism is conceived of solely in terms of helping persons choose to participate in relationships with other believers to the neglect of helping them choose to believe, know, obey, and abide in Jesus.

---

4. Hiebert, *Transforming Worldviews*, 287.

5. Pachuau, "Ethnic Identity," 55–56.

6. Stone, *Evangelism after Christendom*, 10–17.

*The Relational Dimension of Full Life in Christ and Its Impact
on Evangelism Training*

When we understand that the relational dimension of full life in Christ is
integral to full life in Christ, this impacts evangelism training in at least two
ways. First, it influences how the evangelistic vision is conceptualized and
communicated. The relational dimension is included as basic to the evangelistic vision rather than as an extraneous add-on at a later point in the evangelizing or discipling process. Right relationships with other people and
with God's creation are intrinsic to right relationship with God. This is why
the description of the gospel that was given earlier in this chapter referred
to the Christ-following life as "a holistic, *relational* flourishing of persons,
relational networks, communities, and God's creation." My intention here is
not to suggest that the relational dimensions of Christ-following that rise
to the fore in a life-based evangelistic vision are completely missing from
other evangelistic visions. My intention, rather, is simply yet forcefully to
contend that these relational dimensions must be included in the conceptualization, embodiment, and communication of the gospel message if we
are to be faithful to God's full-life intentions for us in Jesus Christ. Thus, for
example, when we engage in evangelism training, one of the "barometer
questions" that we must use is whether the methods of verbal gospel sharing that we teach Christ-followers to use include the relational dimensions
of the Christ-following life.[7] Does the Roman Road reflect these relational
dimensions? Does the Bridge method reflect them? How about the use of
various colors on a bracelet?

Again, let me emphasize that I am not proposing that all other evangelistic visions be discarded in favor of a life-based vision. Rather, I am
proposing that in addition to other methods of gospel sharing, we must
also offer life-based methods that include the relational dimensions.

James Choung's gospel vision demonstrates how the relational dimensions could be included in gospel sharing. He speaks of four aspects of the
essential biblical story: designed for good, damaged by evil, restored for
better, and sent together to heal.[8] His continual focus on relationships,

7. I am using gospel-sharing methods as *one* example of how to apply the essential
point concerning the relational dimensions of a life-based vision of evangelism. This
does not mean, however, that life-based evangelism is limited to verbal or pictorial communication of the gospel message. It is more comprehensive than that, as I have stated
earlier. This issue will be addressed in a subsequent section.

8. Choung, *True Story*, 166.

combined with the fact that we are sent together to heal, provides a good example of what I am encouraging here. The evangelistic community must do more of this type of gospel conceptualization, and we moreover should include life-based references in these conceptualizations rather than limiting most of our references to salvation, kingdom, restoration, and the like.

The relational dimensions of the Christ-following life also impact who we engage in evangelism training. Many training models are designed to equip interested individuals in how to develop relationships with people in their relational networks and then seek appropriate opportunities to share gospel communication and invitation. I strongly applaud these models. Not only do they take seriously the fact that God desires human participation in the evangelizing process, but they also honor the role of relationships in that process. At the same time, though, the tendency with these models is to focus on how individuals can develop relationships with other individuals for evangelizing purposes. The relational dimensions of Christ-following also encourage us to seek better methods and more frequent opportunities for engaging in evangelism training with relational groupings of believers.

Sunday school classes, home groups, congregational-based recreational groups, short-term study groups, families, and informal networks of believers: let us discern ways to help these relational networks of believers learn how to embody and communicate the full-life-in-relationship that God intends and makes possible in Jesus Christ. They are already experiencing the blessing of relationship within their groupings, so it is natural that we equip them to allow the Holy Spirit to use those relational blessings to draw non-believers toward a decision to follow Jesus. Please note that what I envision here is not membership recruitment in order to grow a Sunday school class, but inclusion of the ministry of evangelism within already-existing groups of persons who are experiencing the unparalleled caliber of life that comes through relationship with Jesus and Jesus's followers. As Rick Richardson writes, "God is far more committed to raising up witnessing *communities* than to raising up witnessing *individuals*."[9]

This concludes the most pertinent comments related to the four clusters of original research questions. With these comments, plus the summary description of the research journey provided earlier in this chapter, most of the important evangelistic implications of a strong focus on the biblical theme of life have been covered in depth. Two issues, however, are of sufficient importance in the U.S. American context to merit additional

9. Richardson, *Reimagining Evangelism*, 27.

attention: (1) the relationship of creation care to evangelism, and (2) the relationship of evangelism to the all-dimensions aspect of the Christ-following life.

Creation Care

This issue was treated briefly in chapter 6. The key question at that point was whether it is possible to include creation care as an integral facet of the gospel message without that message becoming overly complex. I withheld judgment to allow for possible insights that might have emerged from the field research, but my preliminary conjecture was that it is indeed possible to include creation care in the gospel message without overcomplicating that message. The field research data did not yield any insight into this issue. However, a brief exploration of Calvin DeWitt's work adds strong support for considering creation care to be an integral part of the biblical story.

DeWitt argues for a return to the biblical perspective that human beings are a part of creation and should not consider themselves as somehow separate from it. He writes that "human beings are part and parcel of God's created order, are God's creatures, embedded in creation."[10] With this foundational understanding, he proceeds to describe three principles that emerge from the Bible. The first is the earth-keeping principle, which refers to our role to "keep and sustain our Lord's creation." The second is the fruitfulness principle, which depicts God's intention that we are to enjoy creation's fruitfulness, but we are not to destroy it. The third is the Sabbath principle, which expresses the necessity for us to provide Sabbath rests for creation. These principles lay the groundwork for what DeWitt terms "God's paradigm of intent," in which he suggests that "the Promised Land with its steward people was the paradigm of intent for the relationship of God, land, and people."[11] This fits well with a life-based evangelistic vision. Not only does it link creation care with God's original intentions in creation, but it also makes reference to the promised land ("a land flowing with milk and honey"), which elicits images of full, vibrant life.

We can confidently affirm my preliminary conjecture and propose that creation care can be included in evangelistic communication without undue complexity or confusion. This is illustrated in the gospel description presented earlier in this chapter, where the life that is experienced through

10. DeWitt, *Just Stewardship*, 22.
11. Ibid., 28–34.

following Christ involves "a holistic and relational flourishing of people, relational networks, communities, and *God's creation*." This inclusion of God's creation in the holistic and relational flourishing that is envisioned as part of the Christ-following life is sufficiently simple and straightforward so as to not unduly complicate the essential gospel message. Moreover, its inclusion opens the door for further exploration into this issue. Given the growing emphasis in the United States on "going green," the inclusion of creation care is not only biblically and theologically faithful, but is also evangelistically wise, for it offers another potential connection point with non-believers.[12]

Following Christ Is to Impact Every Dimension of Our Lives

You will recall that we previously dealt with the issue that following Christ is to impact every dimension of our lives. Building on insights from Jurgen Moltmann, Paul Hiebert, Rene Padilla, Jim Wallis, Leslie Newbigin, and John Wesley, I suggested that evangelistic theory and practice must discover how to prevent persons from making an initial decision to follow Jesus without understanding, appreciating, and committing themselves to the all-dimensions impact that God intends. This is a crucial consideration in any context, but it is especially important in the U.S. American context, where there is a temptation to limit the all-dimensions impact of the Christ-following journey to the individual believer and his or her closest circle of friends. Though this point has been cogently argued already, it would help if we add the thoughts of David Bosch at this juncture.

Bosch proposes that evangelism does indeed share good news of a blessed and gifted life to be experienced in Christ. This life, however, cannot be considered as a private treasure that has no positive impact in the lives of others. Thus, "it is not simply to receive life that people are called to

---

12. An important caveat at this point is that although "going green" has become a stronger focus in the United States in recent years, the commitment to creation care will nevertheless fight a constant uphill battle against the U.S. American cultural tendency to view nature and the environment as something that human beings should control rather than as something that human beings live in vital harmony with. Althen and Bennett (*American Ways*, 16) suggest that this concept is tied to the U.S. American emphasis on the possibility of changing the future by taking action in the present. Based on their belief in the possibility of engendering change through planning and action, U.S. Americans assume "that their physical and social environments are subject to human domination or control."

be Christians, but rather to give life."[13] Germane to the current discussion is that this giving of life is neither viewed nor intended by God to be limited to one-to-one transactions that have little or no impact in public and social spheres. This does not mean that in the midst of personal difficulties it is inappropriate to experience peace, joy, healing, or comfort through the life that Jesus brings. Bosch suggests that it does mean, however, that Jesus offers these positive personal experiences only within the context of "the lordship of Christ in all realms of life, an authoritative word of hope that the world as we know it will not always be the way it is."[14] Grounded in this understanding, then, Bosch contends that evangelism is a call to service: "God wills not only that we be rescued from hell and redeemed for heaven, but also that within us—and through our ministry in society around us—the 'fullness of Christ' be re-created, the image of God be restored in our lives and relationships." In the final analysis, Bosch proposes that "evangelism, then, is calling people to mission."[15] James Choung echoes this perspective when he writes of the early disciples in the gospel narratives: "From the very outset, Jesus invites them to join in his mission—to advance the kingdom he started. From the get-go, Jesus gives them a picture of what it means to serve people and to stop seeking their own self-gratification. He wanted them to look up from the selfishness of their own hearts and to start serving others with love and justice."[16]

This call to serve others with love and justice must be included as an integral component of the gospel message. It is too important to save this dimension of God's intentions for subsequent introduction in the ministry of discipleship. This is especially true in the United States, where there is a strong temptation to privatize the blessings of following Jesus and compartmentalize his teachings in such a way that they impact personal piety but not social, cultural, economic, and political involvement. As Bosch notes: "Preachers steer clear of controversial social issues and concentrate on those personal sins of which most of their enthusiastic listeners are not guilty. However, what criterion decides that racism and structural injustice are social issues but pornography and abortion personal? Why is politics shunned and declared to fall outside of the competence of the evangelist,

---

13. Bosch, *Transforming Mission*, 414.

14. Ibid., 417.

15. Ibid., 417–18.

16. Choung, *True Story*, 160.

except when it favors the position of the privileged in society?"[17] These insights from Bosch, Choung, and many others lead to an improvement of the gospel description given earlier in this chapter. This earlier description suggests that the good news may be viewed as follows:

> Through a full-bodied trust in and following of Jesus, we receive forgiveness and are initiated into a life of wholeness (redemption) and reconciliation. This life is best described as a holistic and relational flourishing of people, relational networks, communities, and God's creation; and this flourishing will be characterized by joy, peace, justice, love, purpose, and provision, in all dimensions of life.

A better description is that the good news may be viewed as follows (additions are italicized):

> Through a full-bodied trust in and following of Jesus, we receive forgiveness and are initiated into a *personal and public* life of wholeness (redemption), reconciliation, and *service*. This life is best described as a holistic and relational flourishing of people, relational networks, communities, and God's creation, *as together we partner with Jesus in his life-giving mission to the world, serving as agents of* joy, peace, *social justice, political justice, economic justice,* love, purpose, and provision, in all *personal and public* dimensions of life.

Because this redacted gospel description is a more faithful representation of the biblical and theological vision of the full life that God intends and offers in Jesus Christ, we should also amend the description of full life that was suggested earlier. The amended description reads as follows, with changes highlighted in italics:

> Life as God intends us to experience it in Jesus is a holistic, relational flourishing of people, relational networks, communities, and God's creation. This life is rooted in a full-bodied trust in and following of Jesus (this includes knowing, obeying, and abiding in him), which brings us forgiveness and initiates a *personal and public* life of wholeness (redemption), reconciliation (with God, ourselves, and others), and *service. Together, we are to partner with Jesus in his life-giving mission to the world, serving as agents of* joy, peace, *social justice, political justice, economic justice,* love, purpose, and provision, in all *personal and public* dimensions of life.

17. Bosch, *Transforming Mission*, 417.

Life-Based Evangelism Ministry Must Have a Broad Scope

The fact that the life just described is possible through following Jesus is the good news that we share through a life-based ministry of evangelism. But what is meant by *share*? Simply put, the foundation of a life-based ministry of evangelism is a comprehensive, broadly-based embodiment of a flourishing life-based Christian identity. This embodiment will include words, but it will also include a portrayal of the varying dimensions of the full life in Christ that God intends for us. As Christ-followers who wish to participate in a life-based ministry of evangelism, therefore, we not only talk about the different dimensions of full life with non-believers, but we also portray those dimensions in our personal lives and in the corporate life of the congregation, so that they may see for themselves how full and vibrant life can be when people follow Jesus.

This portrayal of the fullness of the Christ-following life was mentioned by several interviewees in response to the question, who or what was influential in your initial decision to follow Christ? One interviewee referred to the role models he witnessed in his childhood church.[18] Another person mentioned seeing the impact of Jesus in other people's lives in his youth group.[19] Yet another said that her husband "showed me you can be a follower of Christ and still laugh and have fun."[20] A fourth interviewee spoke of seeing the peace and joy in her brother's face when he chose to follow Jesus.[21] A fifth person referred to "seeing how my mom's life was compared to my other friends and my friends' parents, and I wanted my family to be on a better track than the track my mom's life was on."[22] A sixth respondent talked about "the quality of lives of people who said they followed Jesus."[23] These examples confirm that the nonverbal, experiential portrayal of the life that God intends in Jesus is a powerful dimension of the ministry of evangelism.

This portrayal of the Christ-following life in nonverbal expressions does not, however, mean that verbal communication and invitation are unnecessary. They too are vital dimensions of a comprehensive ministry of

18. Interview with author, Dacula, GA, June 13, 2010.
19. Interview with author, Duluth, GA, April 27, 2010.
20. Interview with author, Loganville, GA, April 26, 2010.
21. Interview with author, Augusta, GA, May 16, 2010.
22. Interview with author, Loganville, GA, April 26, 2010.
23. Interview with author, Mt. Pleasant, SC, June 8, 2010.

evangelism. Language is one of the primary ways we communicate as human beings, and the use of language must therefore be used in the ministry of evangelism. As the Incarnate One, Jesus models this for us quite forcefully. It is true that while on earth Jesus portrayed the life that he intends for us through laughter, sharing of relationships, acts of compassion, healings, miracles of provision, and more. He also, however, invested a great deal of time in preaching and teaching, sharing the message of full life in him through the medium of verbal communication.

An important consideration regarding this point is that we should not make use of language in the ministry of evangelism simply because language is a primary means of communication for human beings. Rather, I would point out that not only does language serve as a medium of communication, but it also influences our conceptualizations. Just as thoughts shape our words, so too do words shape our thoughts. Lakoff and Johnson contend, for example, that there are some metaphors we use in our U.S. American culture that not only express our conceptions of the world, but actually shape those conceptions.[24] I would expand this notion to include not only metaphors but also primary images, and this is one of the reasons I have given many examples throughout this project concerning how to apply a life-based evangelistic vision to the verbal sharing of the gospel message. Without question the ministry of evangelism is not limited to verbal communication. On the other hand, though, since the consistent repetition of metaphors and images can shape our conceptions, it is also true that we will never fully embrace a ministry of life-based evangelism if we do not also embrace new ways of sharing verbal communication and invitation that are consistent with our portrayal of the life that Jesus intends for us. We must walk the life-based walk, *and* we must talk the life-based talk.

The ministry of evangelism, therefore, seeks to (1) embody (portray and verbally communicate) the flourishing life that God intends for us as we follow Jesus; and to (2) invite, guide, lead, encourage, and/or direct nonbelievers toward choosing to follow Jesus and experiencing (and contributing to) that life for themselves and others. Individual Christians, relational groupings of Christians, organized congregations, and other Christian ministry groups should engage in this life-based evangelistic ministry.

---

24. Lakoff and Johnson, *Metaphors We Live By*, 3–6.

Final Thoughts

Life-based evangelism merits a place at the evangelistic table. Along with kingdom-based evangelism, forgiveness-based evangelism, discipleship-based evangelism, and many other evangelistic visions, life-based evangelism has clear biblical warrant. It appropriately highlights God's original intentions in creation and God's new intentions in Jesus Christ. It also appropriately addresses the search for full and meaningful life that many people experience. Without discarding other evangelistic visions that have served us well in the past and will continue to do so in the future, I encourage my fellow Jesus-followers to fully embrace life-based evangelism.

Let us deepen our understanding of the biblical material that underscores God's profound interest in life.

Let us expand our theological and evangelistic vocabulary to include life-based imagery.

Let us learn to embody and articulate God's full-life intentions in a way that helps non-Christians understand them and see them as realistic possibilities for their own lives.

Let us invite them to give a rousing "yes" to God's invitation to experience full life with Jesus and others.

May we offer them life, and may we offer it now.

BIBLIOGRAPHY

Abraham, William. *The Logic of Evangelism*. Grand Rapids: Eerdmans, 1989.

Althen, Gary, and Janet Bennett. *American Ways: A Cultural Guide to the United States.* 3rd ed. Boston: Intercultural, 2011.

Anderson, Ray S. *On Being Human: Essays in Theological Anthropology.* Grand Rapids: Eerdmans, 1982.

Asitimbay, Diane. *What's Up America? A Foreigner's Guide to Understanding Americans.* 2nd ed. San Diego: Culturelink, 2009.

Baab, Otto J. *The Theology of the Old Testament*. New York: Abingdon, 1949.

Baines, John. "Ancient Egyptian Kingship: Official Forms, Rhetoric, Context." In *King and Messiah in Israel and the Ancient Near East*, 46. Edited by John Day. Sheffield, England: Sheffield Academic Press, 1998.

Barr, James. *The Concept of Biblical Theology: An Old Testament Perspective*. London: SCM, 1999.

Barrett, C. K. *The Gospel According to St. John. An Introduction with Commentary and Notes on the Greek Text*. London: S.P.C.K., 1955.

Barth, Karl. "The Doctrine of Creation," *Church Dogmatics* Vol. 2/4. Edited by G.W. Bromiley and T. F. Torrance. Edinburgh: T & T Clark, 1961.

Beasley-Murray, G. R. *Jesus and the Kingdom of God*. Grand Rapids: Eerdmans, 1986.

———. "The Kingdom of God in the Teaching of Jesus." *Journal of the Evangelical Theological Society* 35:1, March (1992) 19.

Bellah, Robert N. "Is There a Common American Culture?" *Journal of the American Academy of Religion* 66, no. 3 (1998) 614–6.

Bock, Darrell. "The Kingdom of God in New Testament Theology." In *Looking Into the Future: Evangelical Studies in Eschatology*, 36. Edited by David W. Baker. Grand Rapids: Baker, 2001.

Bosch, David J. *Transforming Mission: Paradigm Shifts in Theology of Mission*. Maryknoll, NY: Orbis, 1991.

Brown, Michael L. *Israel's Divine Healer: Studies in Old Testament Biblical Theology*. Grand Rapids: Zondervan, 1995.

Brown, Raymond. *The Churches the Apostles Left Behind*. New York: Paulist Press, 1984.

———. *The Community of the Beloved Disciple*. London: Geoffrey Chapman, 1979.

———. *The Gospel According to John (i–xii): Introduction, Translation, and Notes*. Vol. 29 of The Anchor Bible. Edited by William F. Albright and David N. Freedman. Garden City, NY: Doubleday and Company, 1966.

———. *An Introduction to the Gospel of John*. New York: Doubleday, 2003.

Bruce, F. F. *The Gospel of John: Introduction, Exposition, and Notes*. Grand Rapids: Eerdmans, 1983.

Bibliography

Bultmann, Rudolf. "ζαω." In *Theological Dictionary of the New Testament, Volume VI*. Edited by Gerhard Kittel. Translated by Geoffrey W. Bromiley. Grand Rapids: Eerdmans, 1968.

Caragounis, Chrys C. "Kingdom of God/Kingdom of Heaven." In *Dictionary of Jesus and the Gospels*. Edited by Joel B. Green, et al. Downers Grove, IL: InterVarsity, 1992, 417.

Child, Brevard S. *Biblical Theology of the Old and New Testaments: Theological Reflection on the Christian Bible*. Minneapolis: Fortress, 1992.

Choung, James. *True Story: A Christianity Worth Believing In*. Downers Grove, IL: IVP Books, 2008.

Colson, Charles, and Harold Fickett. *The Good Life*. Wheaton: Tyndale, 2005.

Cullman, Oscar. *Christ and Time: The Primitive Conception of Time and History*. Rev. ed. Translated by Floyd V. Filson. Philadelphia: Westminster, 1964.

Danker, Frederick William, editor. *A Greek-English Lexicon of the New Testament and Other Early Christian Literature*. 3rd ed. Chicago: University of Chicago Press, 2000.

Davids, Peter H. "The Kingdom of God Come with Power." *Criswell Theological Review* 2:1, Fall (2004) 19.

Davies, W. D. *The Gospel and the Land: Early Christianity and Jewish Territorial Doctrine*. Berkeley: University of California Press, 1974.

de la Torre, Miguel A. *Reading the Bible from the Margins*. Maryknoll: Orbis, 2002.

de Lourdes, Sister Marie. "Wellsprings of Life." In *The Bible Today*. December (1978) 1825–32.

DeWitt, Calvin B., general editor. *The Just Stewardship of Land and Creation*. Grand Rapids: Reformed Ecumenical Council, 1996.

Dodd, C. H. *The Interpretation of the Fourth Gospel*. Cambridge, England: Cambridge University Press, 1953.

———. *The Parables of the Kingdom*. Rev. ed. New York: Charles Scribner's Sons, 1961.

Dunn, James D. G. *The Theology of Paul the Apostle*. Grand Rapids: Eerdmans, 1998.

Dyck, Drew. *Generation Ex-Christian: Why Young Adults Are Leaving the Faith . . . and How to Bring Them Back*. Chicago: Moody, 2010.

Eichrodt, Walther. *Theology of the Old Testament*, Vol. 1. Translated by J. A. Baker. The Old Testament Library Series. Edited by Peter Ackroyd et al. Philadelphia: Westminster, 1967.

———. *Theology of the Old Testament*, Vol. 2. Translated by J. A. Baker. The Old Testament Library Series. Edited by Peter Ackroyd et al. Philadelphia: Westminster, 1967.

Erickson, Tamara J. *What's Next, Gen X?: Keeping Up, Moving Ahead, and Getting the Career You Want*. Boston: Harvard Business School Publishing, 2010.

Fee, Gordon D. *The Disease of the Health & Wealth Gospels*. Costa Mesa, CA: The Word for Today, 1979.

Finney, Charles G. *Lectures on Revival of Religion*. Edited by William G. McLoughlin. Cambridge, MA: The Belknap Press of Harvard University Press, 1960.

Fischer, Claude S. *Made in America: A Social History of American Culture and Character*. Chicago: University of Chicago Press, 2010.

Gonzalez, Justo. *Faith and Wealth: A History of Early Christian Ideas on the Origin, Significance, and Use of Money*. Eugene: Wipf and Stock, 1990.

Grisez, German. "The True Ultimate End of Human Beings: The Kingdom, Not God Alone," *Theological Studies* 69 (2008) 58–59.

Hanson, Amy. *Baby Boomers and Beyond: Tapping the Ministry Talents and Passions of Adults Over 50*. San Francisco: Jossey-Bass, 2010.

Harink, Douglas. *Paul Among the Postliberals: Pauline Theology Beyond Christendom and Modernity.* Grand Rapids: Brazos, 2003.

Hiebert, Paul G. *Anthropological Insights for Missionaries.* Grand Rapids; Baker Academic, 1985.

————. *Transforming Worldviews: An Anthropological Understanding of How People Change.* Grand Rapids: Baker Academic, 2008.

Houtepen, Anton. "Apocalyptics and the Kingdom of God." *Exchange* 28:4, October (1999) 291–311.

Howe, Neil, and William Strauss. *Millennials Rising: The Next Great Generation.* New York: Vintage Books, 2000.

Hunter, George, III. *The Apostolic Congregation: Church Growth Reconceived for a New Generation.* Nashville: Abingdon, 2009.

————. *Church for the Unchurched.* Nashville: Abingdon, 1996.

————. *How to Reach Secular People.* Nashville: Abingdon, 1992.

Jacob, Edmond. *Theology of the Old Testament.* Translated by Arthur W. Heathcote and Philip J. Allcock. London: Hodder and Stoughton, 1978.

Jagessar, Michael N. *Full Life for All: The Work and Theology of Philip A. Potter. A Historical Survey and Systematic Analysis of Major Themes.* Uitgeverij Boekencentrum: Zoetermeer, 1997.

Jathanna, O. V. "Jesus Christ—The Life of the World: An Indian Christian Understanding." *Indian Journal of Theology* 31:2, Ap–Ju (1982) 78.

John Paul II. *The Gospel of Life [Evangelium Vitae].* New York: Random House, 1995.

John, V. J. "The Concept of 'Life' in the Gospel of John: An Ecological Perspective." *The Indian Journal of Theology* 47:1&2 (2005) 96–97.

Jones, Scott J. *The Evangelistic Love of God and Neighbor: A Theology of Witness and Discipleship.* Nashville: Abingdon, 2003.

Joyce, Paul M. "King and Messiah in Ezekiel." In *King and Messiah in Israel and the Ancient Near East,* 337. Edited by John Day. Sheffield, England: Sheffield Academic Press, 1998.

Kabongo-Mbaya, Philippe B. "Life in Abundance: A Biblical Reflection on John 10:10." *Reformed World* 53:2–3 (2003) 73.

Keller, Timothy. *The Prodigal God: Recovering the Heart of the Christian Faith.* New York: Dutton, 2008.

Kelsey, David H. *Eccentric Existence: A Theological Anthropology.* Louisville: Westminster John Knox Press, 2009.

Kennedy, D. James. *Evangelism Explosion: Equipping Churches for Friendship, Evangelism, Discipleship, and Healthy Growth.* 4th ed. Wheaton, IL: Tyndale House, 1996.

Klein, Hans. "Leben–neues Leben: Moglichkeiten und Grenzen einer gesamtbiblischen Theologies des Alten und Neuen Testaments." *Evangelische Theologie* 43 (1983) 91–107, quoted in Charles H. H. Scobie, "The Structure of Biblical Theology," *Tyndale Bulletin* 42, no. 2 (1991) 177–8.

Koester, Craig R. "The Death of Jesus and the Human Condition: Exploring the Theology of John's Gospel," 141–57. In *Life in Abundance: Studies of John's Gospel in Tribute to Raymond E. Brown, S. S.* Collegeville, MN: Liturgical Press, 2005.

————. *The Word of Life: A Theology of John's Gospel.* Grand Rapids: Eerdmans, 2008.

Kummel, Werner Georg. *Promise and Fulfillment: The Eschatological Message of Jesus.* London: SCM, 1961.

Bibliography

Ladd, George Eldon. *Jesus and the Kingdom: The Eschatology of Biblical Realism*. Waco, TX: Word, 1964.

Lakoff, George, and Mark Johnson. *Metaphors We Live By*. Chicago: University of Chicago Press, 2003.

Lambert, W. G. "Kingship in Ancient Mesopotamia." In *King and Messiah in Israel and the Ancient Near East*, 55. Edited by John Day. Sheffield, England: Sheffield Academic Press, 1998.

Lathem, R. Warren and Dan W. Dunn. *Preaching for a Response*. Anderson, IN: Bristol House, 2008.

Levenson, Jon D. "The Fact of Death and the Promise of Life in Israelite Religion." In *The Papers of the Henry Luce III Fellows in Theology*, Vol. VI, 139–154. Edited by Christopher I. Wilkins. Series in Theological Scholarship and Research. Pittsburgh: The Association of Theological Schools in the United States and Canada, 2003.

Manson, T. W. *On Paul and John: Some Selected Theological Themes*. Studies in Biblical Theology, First (Book 38). Edited by Matthew Black. Naperville, IL: Alec R. Allenson, 1963.

Martens, Elmer A. *God's Design: A Focus on Old Testament Theology*. 3rd ed. North Richland Hills, TN: Bibal, 1998.

McConville, J. G. "King and Messiah in Deuteronomy and the Deuteronomistic History." In *King and Messiah in Israel and the Ancient Near East*, 281. Edited by John Day. Sheffield, England: Sheffield Academic Press, 1998.

McGavran, Donald A. *Understanding Church Growth*. 3rd ed., rev. Edited by C. Peter Wagner. Grand Rapids: Eerdmans, 1980.

McPhee, Arthur G. *Friendship Evangelism: The Caring Way to Share Your Faith*. Grand Rapids: Zondervan, 1978.

Mlakuzhyll, George. *Abundant Life in the Gospel of John*. Delhi: ISPCK, 2007.

Moltmann, Jurgen. *The Church in the Power of the Spirit: A Contribution to Messianic Ecclesiology*. New York: Harper & Row, 1977.

———. *The Passion for Life: A Messianic Lifestyle*. Translated by M. Douglas Meeks. Philadelphia: Fortress, 1978.

———. *The Source of Life: The Holy Spirit and the Theology of Life*. Translated by Margaret Kohl. Minneapolis: Augsburg Fortress, 1997.

Morris, Leon. *The Gospel According to John: The English Text with Introduction, Exposition and Notes*. Grand Rapids: Eerdmans, 1971.

———. *Jesus Is the Christ: Studies in the Theology of John*. Grand Rapids: Eerdmans, 1989.

Moule, C. F. D. "The Meaning of 'Life' in the Gospels and Epistles of St. John." *Theology* 78, March (1975) 122, 124.

Newbigin, Leslie. *Foolishness to the Greeks: The Gospel and Western Culture*. Grand Rapids: Eerdmans, 1986.

———. *The Gospel in a Pluralistic Society*. Grand Rapids: Eerdmans, 1989.

———. *Sign of the Kingdom*. Grand Rapids: Eerdmans, 1980.

O'Day, Gail R. "The Love of God Incarnate: The Life of Jesus in the Gospel of John," 158–67. In *Life in Abundance: Studies of John's Gospel in Tribute to Raymond E. Brown, S. S.* Collegeville, MN: Liturgical Press, 2005.

———. *The Word Disclosed: Preaching the Gospel of John*. St. Louis: Chalice, 2002.

Oden, Thomas C. *Life in the Spirit, Systematic Theology: Volume Three*. New York: Harper Collins, 1992.

———. *The Living God, Systematic Theology: Volume One*. New York: Harper Collins, 1987.

——. *The Word of Life, Systematic Theology: Volume Two.* New York: Harper Collins, 1989.

Oswalt, John. *On Being a Christian: Thoughts from John the Apostle.* Wilmore, KY: Francis Asbury Press, 2008.

——. *Theological Wordbook of the Old Testament,* Vol. 1. Edited by R. Laird Harris. Chicago: Moody Press, 1980.

Outler, Albert. *Evangelism and Theology in the Wesleyan Spirit.* Nashville: Discipleship Resources, 2003.

Pachuau, Lalsangkima. "Ethnic Identity and the Gospel of Reconciliation," *Mission Studies* 26 (2009) 55–56.

Packer, J. I. *Evangelism and the Sovereignty of God.* Downers Grove, IL: IVP Academic, 1961.

Padilla, C. Rene. "Introduction: An Ecclesiology for Integral Mission," 19–49. In *The Local Church, Agent of Transformation: An Ecclesiology for Integral Mission.* Edited by Tetsunao Yamamori and C. Rene Padilla. Buenos Aires: Ediciones Kairos, 2004.

Perrin, Norman. *Jesus and the Language of the Kingdom: Symbol and Metaphor in New Testament Interpretation.* Philadelphia: Fortress, 1976.

Richardson, Rich. *Reimagining Evangelism: Inviting Friends on a Spiritual Journey.* Downers Grove: IVP Books, 2006.

Rooke, Deborah. "Kingship as Priesthood: The Relationship between the High Priesthood and the Monarchy." In *King and Messiah in Israel and the Ancient Near East,* 94. Edited by John Day. Sheffield, England: Sheffield Academic Press, 1998.

Schnackenburg, Rudolf. *The Gospel According to St. John, Volume One: Introduction and Commentary on Chapters 1–4.* New York: Crossroad, 1990.

Schneider, John R. *The Good of Affluence: Seeking God in a Culture of Wealth.* Grand Rapids: Eerdmans, 2002.

Schweitzer, Albert. *The Quest of the Historical Jesus: First Complete Edition.* Edited by John Bowden. London: SCM, 2000.

Scobie, Charles H. H. "The Structure of Biblical Theology." *Tyndale Bulletin* 42, no. 2 (1991) 177.

Sider, Ronald J. *Rich Christians in an Age of Hunger: Moving from Affluence to Generosity.* W Publishing Group, no place given, 1997.

Sleeth, Matthew. "The Power of a Green God," 117–124. In *The Green Bible, NRSV.* San Francisco: HarperCollins, 2008.

Sloyan, Gerard S. *John: Interpretation: A Bible Commentary for Teaching and Preaching.* Atlanta: John Knox, 1988.

Smalley, Stephen S. *John: Evangelist and Interpreter.* London: Paternoster, 1978.

Smith, D. Moody. *The Theology of the Gospel of John, New Testament Theology.* Edited by James D. G. Dunn. Cambridge, England: Cambridge University Press, 1995.

Smith, J. Walker, and Ann Clurman. *Generation Ageless: How Baby Boomers Are Changing the Way We Live Today . . . And They're Just Getting Started.* New York: Harper Collins, 2007.

Snyder, Howard A. "Salvation Means Creation Healed: Creation, Cross, Kingdom, and Mission." *Asbury Journal* 62:1 (Spr 2007) 11.

——. *Yes in Christ: Wesleyan Reflections on Gospel, Mission, and Culture.* Tyndale Studies in Wesleyan History and Theology 2. Edited by Howard A. Snyder. Toronto: Clements Academic, 2011.

Soper, Donald. *The Advocacy of the Gospel.* Nashville: Abingdon, 1961.

Bibliography

Stark, Rodney. *The Rise of Christianity: How the Obscure, Marginal Jesus Movement Became the Dominant Force in the Western World in a Few Centuries.* San Francisco: HarperSanFrancisco, 1996.

Steward, Edward, and Milton Bennett. *American Cultural Patterns: A Cross-Cultural Perspective.* Rev. ed. Boston: Intercultural, 1991.

Stone, Bryan. *Evangelism after Christendom: The Theology and Practice of Christian Witness.* Grand Rapids: Brazos Press, 2007

Sweazey, George E. *Effective Evangelism: The Greatest Work in the World.* New York: Harper and Brothers, 1953.

Taylor, Charles. *A Secular Age.* Cambridge, MA: Belknap, 2007.

Thomas, Richard W. "The Meaning of the Terms 'Life' and 'Death' in the Fourth Gospel and in Paul." *Scottish Journal of Theology* 21:2, June (1968) 204.

Thompson, Marianne. "Eternal Life in the Gospel of John." *Ex auditu* 5 (1989) 35–55.

Wallis, Jim. *The Call to Conversion: Why Faith Is Always Personal but Never Private.* Rev. ed. San Francisco: HarperSanFrancisco, 2005.

Waltke, Bruce. "The Kingdom of God in Biblical Theology." In *Looking Into the Future: Evangelical Studies in Eschatology*, 15–27. Edited by David W. Baker. Grand Rapids: Baker, 2001.

Wesley, John. "Christian Perfection." In *The Works of John Wesley, Vol. VI.* 3rd ed. Grand Rapids: Baker, 1979.

———. Sermon 24, "Upon Our Lord's Sermon on the Mount." In *Wesley's Fifty-Two Standard Sermons.* Edited by N. Burwash. Nicholasville, KY: Schmul Publishing, 1988.

———. *The Works of John Wesley, Vol. V.* 3rd ed. Grand Rapids: Baker, 1979.

Westermann, Claus. *Blessing in the Bible and the Life of the Church.* Philadelphia: Fortress, 1978.

———. *What Does the Old Testament Say About God?* Edited by Friedemann W. Golka. Atlanta: John Knox, 1979.

Whitelam, Keith W. *The Just King: Monarchical Judicial Authority in Ancient Israel.* Sheffield, England: JSOT, 1979.

Whybray, R. Norman. *The Good Life in the Old Testament.* London: T & T Clark, 2002.

Willard, Dallas. *The Divine Conspiracy: Rediscovering Our Hidden Life in God.* San Francisco: HarperSanFrancisco, 1998.

Witherington, Ben III. *John's Wisdom: A Commentary on the Fourth Gospel.* Louisville, KY: Westminster John Knox, 1995.